Speak it out until I rise above the lies
Speak it out until my soul is satisfied
So I'll speak Your name, speak Your name

'Cause I believe who You say You are
I can see the goodness of Your heart
I won't live by what the world will say
I'll speak Your name, speak Your name

Jesus, Jesus, Jesus
Jesus, Jesus, Jesus
Jesus, my Papa, Jesus, my Friend, Jesus
Jesus, my Healer, Jesus, my Life, Jesus

'Cause I believe who You say You are
I can see the goodness of Your heart
I won't live by what the world will say
I'll speak Your name, speak Your name

– *SPEAK YOUR NAME,*
by Laney Rene

SPEAK YOUR NAME
Devotions and Declarations on the Reality of Jesus

Copyright © 2020 Laney Rene

ISBN: 978-1-951701-00-0

Published by Breakfast for Seven, a division of Inprov LLC, 2150 E. Continental Blvd., Southlake, TX, 76092.

Distributed by Thomas Nelson.

Unless otherwise noted, all scripture quotations are taken from the New King James Version®. Copyright © 1982 by Thomas Nelson. Used by permission. All rights reserved.

Scripture quotations marked (NIV) are taken from the Holy Bible, New International Version®, NIV®. Copyright © 1973, 1978, 1984, 2011 by Biblica, Inc.™ Used by permission of Zondervan. All rights reserved worldwide. www.zondervan.com

Scripture quotations marked (TPT) are taken from The Passion Translation®. Copyright © 2017, 2018 by Passion & Fire Ministries, Inc. Used by permission. All rights reserved. ThePassionTranslation.com.

Scripture quotations marked (ESV) are taken from the English Standard Version® (ESV®), Copyright ©2001 by Crossway, a publishing ministry of Good News Publishers. All rights reserved.

Printed in the United States of America.

LANEY RENE

SPEAK YOUR NAME

Devotions and Declarations on the Reality of Jesus

**BREAKFAST
FOR SEVEN**

HOW TO USE QR CODES

Hey friend! Before we go any further, there's a tool I want to give you that will help you enjoy this devotional to the fullest. Throughout the devotional, you will find QR codes. A QR code looks like this:

Your smart phone camera may have a built-in reader to scan this code but if not, no worries . . . simply head to the app store on your phone and download a QR reader for free. (If you search for "QR Reader" in the app store, a number of options should come up.)

Once downloaded, open the QR reader and point the camera on your phone at the QR code in the devotional. The app will then ask you to open the linked web page in a browser. Once the web page has opened, you'll see the video.

I hope each message brings you more life and encouragement as you read!

CONTENTS

FOREWORD

I first met Laney in a dressing room on a music tour in 2017. She knocked on the door while I was in there alone, dancing by myself to get the nerves out before speaking. I was going to invite her to my personal dance party right then and there, but we ended up having one of the deepest conversations I've ever had with a stranger. We talked about boys, relationships, struggles, wants, wishes, and all the things. We quickly bonded over our boy talk, our stellar dance moves (hers a little better than mine), but more than that, we bonded over the season of life we were in and how good Jesus was to both of us.

It wasn't long before we ended up being the best of friends and then decided to be roommates. We would stay up till 2 AM on regular occasions talking on the couch, eating popcorn or Halo Top Ice Cream. The odds are we were probably making some kind of funny video. We called our couch "The Pit," because it was just a giant place of fluff, and that is where at least 50 percent of our friendship was spent. We would share nightly recaps about our dates, some good and some not so good, until we found our incredible husbands.

Laney and I decided to pray that we would meet our husbands at the same time, and sure enough God did His thing. Laney met Clayton on mine and Christian's first date. And yes, she was there. They got married two weeks after us and we have remained bonded over the same season of life, our new husbands, and our love for Jesus.

Honestly, there were moments of laughter, moments of crazy random dancing, moments of conviction, moments of forgiveness, moments of prayer, moments of praise, and moments where we had to ask each other the hard questions in life. From snot-faced tears to the most hilarious memories, we really walked a lot of life together during that season. If "The Pit" could talk, it would have a lot to share. Lucky for us, it can't.

Looking back at that time of life when Laney and I lived together and not only did everyday life together but every second, I can say that was when I began my closest relationship with Jesus. We both met at His love every day and shared the things He was doing in our life. We celebrated the little and the big things He did.

We pushed each other in the things God placed in front of us no matter how scared we were, and we were determined to help each other's faith grow. I remember one time before I started touring, I began to get really nervous and felt like I could not do it. Laney walked over to me when others were giving me sympathy and she said, "NO NO NO NO NO NO NO! You will not do this. Look how much Jesus has done in you." She would not let me sit in fear. She always called me to faith.

There is something powerful and important about having a friend who pushes you to His life for you and His purposes for you.

Speak Your Name is like a conversation with a close friend on "The Pit." I promise you one thing, Laney will always lead you to the love of Jesus. I believe that through the Spirit, these words and prayers will meet you in the season that you are in. Her words have come straight from her heart, to you as a friend, onto the pages of this devotional. I know that because everything she does comes straight from her heart. I will tell you, her way of loving is to tell you the truth, challenge you, and push you to your fullness in Him. Get comfy, open your heart, laugh at yourself, and be willing to be challenged and encouraged by Laney's lead and Jesus' love. ◊

Sadie Robertson Huff

INTRODUCTION

Though we are "in" this world, if we believe in the name of Jesus, we are no longer "of" this world. We have been adopted into His kingdom and His kingdom is our new reality. This world is often run by systems, diagnoses, status, and statistics, but we were created for a new kingdom and a new reality.

This new reality is found in one name, Jesus. Jesus came to the world and showed us a new and better way of life. This new life revolves around Him, involves Him, and reveres Him more than any other name that is to be named.

Have you ever noticed how easily we receive the names the world gives us? Whether it be anxiety, fear, depression, sickness, or disease, we seem to accept these things so easily. We often wear these names and labels around like they are our identity.

We hide in our anxiety and sometimes even find comfort in the fact that we have an answer for our problems, but these things were never meant to be the answer. Anxiety is not our destiny. Fear is not our God-given identity. Depression is not the end for us.

Jesus said, "I am the way, the truth, and the life" (John 14:6). I'm sure we've all probably heard this verse before, but oh how easily we forget it. He is our truth, and what He has spoken over us and called us into is greater than any other name we could ever be given. Not only is He our truth, but He is our LIFE. Philippians 2:9–11 says,

> *Therefore God also has highly exalted Him and given Him the name which is above EVERY name, that at the name of Jesus every knee should bow, of those in heaven, and of those on earth, and of those under the earth, and that every tongue should confess that Jesus Christ is Lord, to the glory of God the Father* (emphasis added).

His name is above the name of cancer, fear, anxiety, depression, and every name that is to be named. At the name of Jesus, anxiety will bow, fear will go, depression will be no more, and even cancer will dissolve. Nothing is stronger and more powerful than the name of Jesus.

So, let's speak His name instead of the names of fear, sickness, disease, lack, depression, guilt, and shame. Jesus! He is the better way that we have been searching for. Jesus! His name is what is true. Jesus! His name is LIFE. ◊

Laney Rene

JESUS

My Authority

"Behold, I give you the authority to trample on serpents and scorpions, and over all the power of the enemy, and nothing shall by any means hurt you."

LUKE 10:19 NKJV

Can you remember the last time you said, "I have a headache"? Or maybe the last time you said, "I have anxiety, fear, or a certain sickness or disease?" Have you ever thought about how easily we say we "have" these things that are not eternal before we realize and speak over ourselves the things that are? Why does it often feel easier to say what the world tells us we have before we're able to say what Jesus tells us we have?

Jesus said in Luke 10:19, "Behold, I give you the authority to trample on serpents and scorpions, and over all the power of the enemy, and nothing shall by any means hurt you." Think about a serpent and a scorpion. Jesus has given us authority over them both, but what is it that they both have in common? They both inject venom. Venom is poison that if not retracted will gradually take over the whole body and can eventually end in death. Could it be that these words we so easily accept, that are not life and truth, act as poison to our body? Could it be that we often speak words of death over ourselves without even realizing it? And yet our heavenly Father is saying, "I have given you authority over these things!"

May today be the start and the day we realize what we truly "have" and have freely been given by Jesus, simply by the power that His name carries. Before we say, "I have a headache," what if we said, "I know I have healing, because Jesus has given me authority over all the power of the enemy." Before we say, "I have anxiety," what if we said, "I feel overwhelmed with worry and anxiousness, but I know through Jesus I have authority over these feelings, and they will not control me."

Recognizing the authority we have in Jesus will change the way we see our situations or receive bad news, because we know that these things are not what is final or eternal. Jesus is final. His death and His resurrection are the final words in your life. His death and His resurrection are where sickness, fear, anxiety, depression, doubt, insecurity, and lack were forever finished. In every moment, live in the authority of the One who defeated every form of death. ◊

DECLARATION *Prayer*

Jesus, You Are My Authority.
In Your name, I know I have the authority to speak life over any situation and believe that it can and will change. I believe that through Your name, I have authority over everything the enemy means for harm in my life. Help me to speak Your name before I speak the things of this world over my life. May Your goodness and the truth of Your name be on my lips today. In Jesus' name; Amen.

My Everything

———————

And he asked them, "But who do you say that I am?" Peter answered him, "You are the Christ."

MARK 8:29 ESV

" Jesus, You are my everything." Have you ever said those words before? Although this is a true statement, do you realize just how true these words are? If Jesus is truly your everything, that means absolutely *everything!*

One day, when Jesus was walking with His disciples to the towns of Caesarea Philippi, He asked them, "'Who do men say that I am?' So they answered, 'John the Baptist; but some say, Elijah; and others, one of the prophets'" (Mark 8:27–28).

I imagine Jesus' heart must've sunk in that moment, hearing that everyone thought He was someone or something that He wasn't. He was Jesus, the Son of God; still people misunderstood Him. I wonder how often we do this today, even those of us who believe in His name. I wonder where we have missed His heart and misunderstood what He came to do.

After Jesus heard His disciples say who people say He is, He turned to them and asked, "Who do you say that I am?" (Mark 8:29). Have you ever stopped and asked yourself who Jesus is to you? Yes, He is everything, but what is "everything"?

For the people of Jesus' hometown of Nazareth, He was the carpenter's son, Mary's son, the brother of James, Joseph, Simon, and Judas (see Matthew 13:55–56). The people of Nazareth saw Jesus in the natural and were not able to see Him as God in the flesh. Due to their unbelief that He was the Son of God, Jesus was not able to do many miracles there (see Matthew 13:58).

Although what they believed didn't change who Jesus was,

it did determine what they received from Him. There is so much power in "who" you believe Jesus is. Many people see Jesus of Nazareth as a good person who led an exemplary life. They feel that if we could all just live a little more like Him, the world would be a better place. They don't see Him as the Bread of Life or the One who came to give them living water so that they would never thirst again.

Jesus didn't just come to set a good example; He IS the example. He's not just a good person that we look up to; He IS our only goodness. In His own words, He describes Himself as "the way, the truth, and the life" (John 14:6).

Just as Jesus said to the centurion in Matthew 8:13, "As you have believed, so let it be done for you."

> If you see Jesus as your Provider,
> you will see Him be your Provider.
>
> If you see Jesus as your Healer,
> you will see Him be your Healer.
>
> If you see Him as your Comforter,
> you will be comforted by Him.

Jesus is everything. May we see Him as everything, every day and in every moment. ◊

DECLARATION *Prayer*

Jesus, You Are My Everything.
Show me what it means to see You as absolutely everything in my life. I believe in the fullness of who You are and want to experience You in every area. I believe You are where my help comes from. I believe You are the water that never runs dry. I believe You satisfy every part of me. I believe You are the Son of God who loves me and came to earth for me. Thank You for who You are. In Jesus' name; Amen.

JESUS

My Hope

. . . but those who hope in the
LORD will renew their strength.
They will soar on wings like eagles;
they will run and not grow weary,
they will walk and not be faint.

ISAIAH 40:31, NIV

It can be incredibly hard, when we feel like God has given us a promise, not to start hoping in the promise rather than the One who gave us the promise. It's so easy to get caught in a cycle of trying to make things happen for ourselves rather than realizing that God works best while we rest.

Psalm 127:1–2 (NLT) says,

> Unless the Lord builds a house, the work of the builders is wasted. Unless the Lord protects a city, guarding it with sentries will do no good. It is useless for you to work so hard from early morning until late at night, anxiously working for food to eat; for God gives rest to his loved ones.

In our humanness, this doesn't make sense. It seems that we must work in order to make our way, but in God's kingdom things often work opposite of the world. So, instead of striving to make everything go the way you think it should, let's try a new approach together!

Today, let's rest. Take a deep breath in, and remember what was done for you and the love that has been lavished upon you through Jesus. God sent His Son to be the HOPE of the world. Isaiah 40:31 says,

> ". . . but those who hope in the LORD will renew their strength. They will soar on wings like eagles; they will run and not grow weary, they will walk and not be faint" (NIV).

Imagine how hard it must've been for Abraham to put his hope in God when God asked him to sacrifice Isaac.

Isaac was the promise Abraham had been waiting and hoping for his whole life, and then God asked him to kill his only, promised son.

How was Abraham able to obey this kind of command? Imagine if you prayed for something your whole life, you put all your hope in that one thing happening one day, and then God says, "Hey, remember how I promised you that dream? Well, I want you to let go of it. And not only do I want you to let it go, but I want you to kill it." I can't imagine how hard this must've been for Abraham, or maybe it wasn't hard for him at all. Hebrews 11 tells us that Abraham trusted that if God was faithful to give him Isaac, He would be faithful to give him back.

Abraham didn't place his hope in the promise. Abraham didn't hope in Isaac. Abraham knew that his hope was in God. We cannot lose hope when our hope rests in the One who created us. And if you know this story, you know that Abraham's hope in God was not disappointed. God provided a ram just in time! He wasn't early or a moment late, but right on time. Real hope is found where real hope cannot ever be lost—in Jesus. He is our hope and the hope of the whole world. ◊

DECLARATION *Prayer*

Jesus, You Are My Hope.

I don't want to hope in my own efforts or ability. I want to put my hope in You. Help me to remember Your goodness and the free gift and hope of my salvation. You are my one true hope in this life. I trust You. I let go of my striving to survive and lean into the rest You have for me. You are my sure hope and foundation. In Your name I pray. Thank you, Jesus!

JESUS
My Life

"For My flesh is food indeed, and My blood is drink indeed. He who eats My flesh and drinks My blood abides in Me, and I in him. As the living Father sent Me, and I live because of the Father, so he who feeds on Me will live because of Me. This is the bread which came down from heaven— not as your fathers ate the manna, and are dead. He who eats this bread will live forever."

JOHN 6:55–58 NKJV

We live in a world where we're often told many things are our source of life. Whether it's a new product that promises life-changing results or a new prescription that assures a cure, we must know that these things are not truly our source of life. Yes, God can use anything. He can make the rocks cry out and worship Him (see Luke 19:40), and He uses the foolish things of the world to shame the wise (see 1 Corinthians 1:27). Though God can use anything and anyone, nothing is meant to be our source of true life other than Jesus.

In John 6:47–48 Jesus said, "Most assuredly, I say to you, he who believes in Me has everlasting life. I am the bread of life." Oh, how simple this is, yet we can often find ourselves running around like a dog without a leash trying to find fresh water. We often chase things that we think will satisfy, fix, sustain or protect us, but what we're truly looking for is Jesus: the true Bread of Life, the true satisfier of our souls, and the only One who sustains us.

Look at the Israelites as they fled Egypt. While they were in the wilderness, God sent down manna from heaven for them to eat. The manna satisfied their hunger but in the end, the people died. Manna did not give them eternal life, even though God used manna to satisfy their hunger. In Exodus 16:32 Moses said, "This is the thing which the LORD has commanded: 'Fill an omer with it [manna], to be kept for your generations, that they may see the bread with which I fed you in the wilderness, when I brought you out of the land of Egypt.'" This is such a beautiful and perfect picture of what the manna truly was for: "that they may see the bread with which I fed you in the wilderness, when I brought you out of the land of Egypt." The manna was always meant to point to the only One who truly gives life.

Jesus is our life. Though daily He provides for us like manna from heaven, may we always see that it is Him and Him alone who is our everlasting life. ◊

What we're truly looking for is **Jesus**: *the true Bread of Life.*

DECLARATION *Prayer*

Jesus, You Are My Life.

Help me run to You before I run to any other thing. You are the Bread of Life and the only One who truly gives life to my mind, body, and soul. Nothing can satisfy me like You do. Fill me up today with all that You are. Help me to see every good thing You are doing, recognize that it is from You, and be grateful. In Your name; Amen!

JESUS

My Reason to Believe

For God has not given us a
spirit of fear, but of power and
of love and of a sound mind.

2 TIMOTHY 1:7 NKJV

The opposite of a spirit of power is a spirit of fear. The opposite of a spirit of love is a spirit of fear. And, the opposite of a sound mind is a spirit of fear.

Power, love, and a sound mind are all given to us by the Holy Spirit. The three words in this verse that describe the Spirit that is living within us are compared to only one word that is opposite of them—fear. To operate in fear is to operate opposite of the Holy Spirit and opposite of who we truly are.

It is no accident that the most often repeated command in Scripture is, "Do not fear." God knows the battle that is in front of you. And He knows what the enemy is using to try to cripple you and keep you in a place of defeat.

Mark 5 and Luke 8 tell the story of a Jewish official named Jairus who pleaded with Jesus to come with him to his home to heal his daughter who was at the point of death. Jesus immediately went with Jairus, but on their way to his home it says that some people reported to Jairus that his daughter had died. Hearing the news, Jesus said, "Do not be afraid; only believe, and she will be made well." When Jesus got to the girl, He took her hand and said, *"Talitha koum!"* (which means "Little girl, I say to you, get up!"), and immediately the girl stood up and began to walk around.

This story is amazing because even after hearing that the girl had died, Jesus tells Jairus to not fear and just believe. Jesus' response was as if the news of the girl's death didn't even touch Him. He wasn't surprised, nor was He afraid. Jesus knew the power that He carried. He knew that He could only speak a word and the young girl would come back to life.

Maybe like Jairus, you've recently received some extremely hard news. Maybe it feels like there's no way out of your current situation. Today, I believe Jesus says to you, "Daughter/Son, do not be afraid; just believe." ◊

DECLARATION *Prayer*

Jesus, You Are My Reason to Believe.

Even when I receive news of death, discouragement, or defeat, I know that Your Word is final, and Your Word is life to me. Even though it may look like there's no reason to believe, I still choose to believe and not fear, for You are with me. You have given me a spirit of power, love, and a sound mind: power, to speak life where there seems to be death; love, that dispels all my fears; and a sound mind, that believes and trusts in Your name. Thank you, Jesus. I receive from You my reason to believe. In Your name I pray; Amen.

JESUS

My Provider

———

*Then they said to Him,
"What shall we do, that we may
work the works of God?" Jesus
answered and said to them,
"This is the work of God, that you
believe in Him whom He sent."*

JOHN 6:28–29 NKJV

Human nature often tells us we must "do," or we must "go," but what if we truly realized our job is just to "believe." Do you ever feel like you're just trying to survive, like responsibilities are piling up and there never seems to be enough time in the day to get done what needs to get done? Do you feel like your efforts are never good enough, or you're just on the edge of failure day after day? This way of life is exhausting, but it is not the way God intended for you to live.

When we hear the word "work," we often hear "do;" but John 6:28–29 tells us that to do the works of God is just to "believe" in whom He sent—Jesus! Could it be that there is more to Jesus and His heart to provide, fill, and do for us than we've ever realized?

John 6:35 says, "I am the bread of life. He who comes to Me shall never hunger, and he who believes in Me shall never thirst." Oftentimes when we hear this verse, I think we interpret it as the satisfying of the hunger and thirst of souls, but Jesus wants to do both. He wants to satisfy our souls as well as satisfy and provide for our physical needs!

In John 6:1–14, we see a beautiful picture of this. Jesus is speaking to five thousand hungry people and has them all sit down. He takes five loaves and two fish that a young boy had and multiplies them till everyone eats, is satisfied, and there were still leftovers. Yes, this was a miracle, but miracles aren't just miracles.

Miracles loudly show the heart of Jesus. Jesus wants to take the little that we have and multiply it. He wants to satisfy us in every way. And His desire is that we will always have some left over.

We weren't made for striving and trying to make it through life hanging on by a thread. Just like in John 6, Jesus is asking you to sit down and rest while He provides for you. ◊

DECLARATION *Prayer*

Jesus, You Are My Provider.

I thank You that You want to provide for me while I rest. Help me to sit down while You work on my behalf. I believe You will provide more than enough. I believe Your desire is to satisfy all my needs. Help me to believe fully in who You are and all that You want to do for me. In Your name; Amen.

JESUS

My Carrier

"Listen to Me, O house of Jacob, and all the remnant of the house of Israel, who have been upheld by Me from birth, who have been carried from the womb: even to your old age, I am He, and even to gray hairs I will carry you! I have made, and I will bear; even I will carry, and will deliver you."

ISAIAH 46:3–4 NKJV

Have you ever thought about how you got here? Not specifically how you got to where you're at in this world, but actually how you got to the world in the first place? What did you have to do with being born? What did you have to do with your parents meeting, and what did they have to do with their parents meeting and so forth? When you think about it, it's pretty amazing to realize how much God carried us and made a way for us before we could ever do a single thing for ourselves.

What is it that tells us that once we become adults, we must carry ourselves, carry our burdens, and carry our family's burdens? When did we start believing we're on our own? This is not the way we were brought into this world, so why is it often the way we try to make it through?

Listen to Him, you who have been upheld by HIM from birth. You have been carried from the womb. Even to your old age, HE will carry you! He has made you, and He will carry you and deliver you. The Father's heart is displayed so beautifully and so clearly through every detail of Creation. You can see His desire to carry you simply through the way He gave you life. Life is a gift that none of us did anything to earn, yet we can freely receive it. Jesus wants to carry you, provide for you, and sustain you just as He did for you while you were in your mother's womb.

You are not on your own; you're being carried. You are held by Him. His arms are wrapped around you and He is holding you up. Your Jesus is the One who has been carrying you all along. Don't fear tomorrow, for even then He promises He will still be carrying you. ◊

DECLARATION *Prayer*

Jesus, You Are My Carrier.

You have been carrying me from before I was born. I know You want to carry me though life; that has always been Your heart. I cannot carry the weight of life on my own. I need You and want You. Jesus, I give you everything. I believe You have rest for my soul. In Your name; Amen.

JESUS
My Power

Faith in Jesus' name has healed this man standing before you. It is the faith that comes through believing in Jesus' name that has made the crippled man walk right in front of your eyes!

ACTS 3:16 TPT

In Acts chapter 3, we see a man who had been crippled from birth being carried and placed at the entrance of the temple. He was often brought there to beg for money. On this particular day, the man who had been crippled from birth encountered Peter and John, reaching out and begging them for money. "Then Peter said, 'I don't have money, but I'll give you this—by the power of the name of Jesus Christ of Nazareth, stand up and walk!' . . . The man jumped up, stood there for a moment stunned, and then began to walk around" (Acts 3:6-8, TPT).

Why didn't Peter just say, "Get up and walk!"? Or why didn't he say, "By the power of my own name, Peter, stand up and walk!"? The reason is because there was no power in the name of Peter; just like there is no power in the name of Bob, Sally, Jan, or Judy. The only reason the man was able to get up and walk was because of the power of the name of Jesus!

But what makes the name of Jesus so powerful? It's "who" He is. The name of Jesus represents and carries the person of Jesus: the One who takes away the sins of the world, raises the dead to life, and heals the blind. All you have to do is read the Gospels to see the power of Jesus. Matthew, Mark, Luke, and John are full of the miracles of Jesus and the fruit of who He was and still is today.

When you pray for healing, do you realize what authority you come in when you come in the name of Jesus? Do you realize just by speaking His name you're breathing life into the atmosphere? What is it today that you need to speak the power of His name over? Is it a relationship that you need Him to resurrect back to life? Is it a symptom you've been having that needs to bow to His name? No matter what it is, you can know that when you speak His name over it, it is already finished. Because of Jesus, because of the price that He paid and the love that He poured out, you can boldly come to His throne of grace and believe that you will receive what you ask for. ◊

Do you realize what authority
you come in when you come
in the name of **Jesus***?*
. . . just by speaking His name
you're breathing life into
the atmosphere . . .

DECLARATION *Prayer*

Jesus, You Are My Power.
Through You, I know I have the power to bring dead things back to life. Through Your name, I have the power to speak things into existence that are not yet seen. Jesus, because of the price You paid and the love You have lavished on me, I know You've given me the same power that caused the crippled man to jump to his feet. I speak Your name over every dead thing and area of my life. I believe in the fullness of Your resurrection power. Thank You, Jesus!

JESUS

My Advocate

---

*. . . And if anyone sins, we
have an Advocate with the Father,
Jesus Christ the righteous.*

1 JOHN 2:1 NKJV

If I took the next few minutes to try and convince you that you had an accuser, for most of us it probably wouldn't take much convincing, if any. Most of us are highly aware that we often feel accused and that there is an evil one behind all the accusations. I once read this quote in *Waking the Dead* by John Eldredge, "The story of your life is the story of the long and brutal assault on your heart, by the one who knows what you can be and fears it." Meaning, the enemy is always assaulting you and accusing you; his goal is to destroy your heart and steal your life.

Why does the enemy want to ruin your life? And why does he want to destroy your heart? Because of the One, Jesus, who lives inside of you. The enemy wants to destroy your life because he wants to destroy Jesus. The beautiful news though is this, you have an Advocate who has already won every battle for you. The accuser will always come to accuse, but if you recognize that you have an Advocate who makes you forever victorious and righteous, you will live undefeated.

Look at the woman who was caught in adultery in John chapter eight. The woman was brought before Jesus by the religious leaders just after being caught in the very act of her sin. The religious leaders must've thought that Jesus would condemn the woman, but instead Jesus turned the focus off the woman's sin by saying to her accusers, "He who is without sin among you, let him throw a stone at her first." Then those who heard Jesus say this, being convicted by their own conscience, left one by one leaving the woman alone with Jesus. Jesus, seeing that no one was left standing with them, asks the woman, "Woman, where are those accusers of yours? Has no one condemned you?" She replied, "No one, Lord." And Jesus said to her, "Neither do I condemn you; go and sin no more" (see John 8:1–11).

Just like in this story, your accusers may disguise themselves as the righteous ones. The accusations you hear in your heart and your mind all day long may sound incredibly true. In fact, they may even be true. Just like the woman caught in adultery, maybe you keep finding yourself in the very act of your sin. Maybe you keep going back to the thing you said you'd never go back to. Friend, the good news is, even when you are rightly accused, your Jesus doesn't accuse you. Even when you are wrong, even when you're in the very act of your sin, Jesus says to you, "Neither do I condemn you; go and sin no more."

Jesus is your Advocate. He is the One who is standing between you and your accusers. The enemy of your heart may tell you that Jesus is the one accusing you, but Jesus can only convict you of your righteousness. He no longer sees any blemish and to Him, "there is no flaw in you" (Song of Songs 4:7, NIV). ◊

DECLARATION *Prayer*

Jesus, You Are My Advocate.

You are the One standing between me and my accusers. I thank You that even when I'm caught in the very act of sin, You don't condemn me. I thank You that You've forever called me "righteous." Help me to recognize the voice of the accuser when he comes to condemn my heart. Convict me again of my righteousness in You today. In Jesus' name; Amen.

JESUS

My Confidence

---

*In the fear of the Lord there is
strong confidence, and His children
will have a place of refuge.*

PROVERBS 14:26 NKJV

When we hear the word "fear" it's usually used in terms of being afraid of something, but did you know there is a kind of fear that brings life?

The fear that Proverbs 14:26 is talking about is the fear of the Lord. This fear doesn't mean to be afraid of God, but it's the kind of fear that reveres and stands in awe of Him more than anything or anyone else. It's a fear and confidence that knows His Word is final and more powerful than anything else. This kind of fear produces supernatural confidence that will truly transform our lives as well as the lives of those around us.

A perfect example of this confidence is found in 1 Samuel 17, the story of David and Goliath. David didn't look at the natural. David had a supernatural confidence from God. When the Israelites were faced with Goliath, every one of them were terrified and afraid, except for David. David didn't fear man. David's confidence was rooted in God, the One he knew had been fighting for him every day.

If you've never heard the story of David and Goliath, it ends with David slaying the giant that everyone feared with just a slingshot and stone. David didn't show up with an army. He didn't even wear battle armor for that matter. But He did show up with great confidence.

What the Israelites didn't know about David is that part of his job tending to sheep meant he was killing lions and bears with his bare hands. Day after day, David had seen the God of Israel give him strength to fight the lion and the bear, protect him, and be his refuge. David's place of surrender and trust in God produced the confidence he needed to defeat the giant in front of him.

This is the confidence you have in Jesus. No matter what giant may come, you need not fear it. Simply speak the name of Jesus. ◊

DECLARATION *Prayer*

Jesus, You Are My Confidence.
Help me to fear Your name above every other name that is to be named. The giant of the fear of man has no hold on me. The giant of doubt and insecurity has no hold on me. You are my confidence and my refuge. Thank You, Jesus!

JESUS
My Rest

"Come to Me, all you who labor and are heavy laden, and I will give you rest. Take My yoke upon you and learn from Me, for I am gentle and lowly in heart, and you will find rest for your souls. For My yoke is easy and My burden is light."

MATTHEW 11:28–30 NKJV

Are you tired, burned out, or weary from life? Do you constantly feel like you're going from one thing to the next just trying to make it through? Do you know that you weren't meant to live like this? Jesus is holding rest in His hands, and He's reaching out to give it to you. All you have to do is receive.

There's so much Jesus died to give us that oftentimes the idea of "rest" can be overlooked. Rest just sounds so uneventful and simple that we think, *But don't I need to do something?* Why is it that we feel we must earn the things that Jesus died and rose to freely give us? The truth is, God works best while we REST. We often think that if we try harder, work longer hours, and strive to be a little bit better of a person, we will accomplish more; but that is not the life that Jesus desires for us.

Jesus said, "Come to Me." Jesus isn't asking for our "try harder" or our "do better," He simply wants us to "come" and let Him "do."

Psalm 127:1–2 says, "If God's grace doesn't help the builders, they will labor in vain to build a house. If God's mercy doesn't protect the city, all the sentries will circle it in vain. It really is senseless to work so hard from early morning till late at night, toiling to make a living for fear of not having enough. God can provide for his lovers even while they sleep!" (TPT).

Beloved, God can provide for you even while you sleep! You don't have to strive to carry your burden, for Jesus wants to take your burden and give you His own. And His burden is easy, and it is light. ◊

DECLARATION *Prayer*

Jesus, You Are My Rest.

You are the One who holds me and keeps me. Thank You that You want to take my heavy burdens and give me Your own, which is easy and light. I don't want to strive to do better, but simply want to receive from Your hand all that You have for me. Thank You, Jesus!

JESUS
My Friend

———————

"No longer do I call you servants, for a servant does not know what his master is doing; but I have called you friends, for all things that I heard from My Father I have made known to you."

JOHN 15:15 NKJV

If you're honest, when you think of your relationship with Jesus do you see yourself more as a servant or as a friend? When you think of Jesus, do you see Him as your Master who gives you orders or as the Friend who satisfies your soul? Way too often, we don't realize that what we need and desire most, we already have in Jesus.

Jesus said to the disciples in John 15:15, "No longer do I call you servants," because Jesus desired relationship with them. We can see His heart so clearly in the way that He came down from heaven to be where we are, so that He could do real, everyday life with us. Jesus doesn't want weekend "duty;" He wants our hearts. Have you ever had a friend that made you feel like by spending time with you they were doing you a favor? Like maybe they spend time with you because they feel like they have to, rather than actually want to. This is the way many of us feel in our relationship to Jesus, because our idea of relationship has always been "duty" rather than true desire.

In Matthew 9:10–12, we see that when Jesus sat down at a table with His disciples, many tax collectors and sinners came to sit down with Him. Take a minute to think about how approachable Jesus must have been that the people who were usually known as outcasts would just go take a seat by Him. The tax collectors and the sinners were those who the religious people didn't think Jesus should be sitting with, much less be friends with. Jesus was not like the Pharisees or the religious people. The Pharisees and religious people wanted others to respect them from a distance, but Jesus wanted to be in close relationship.

When the Pharisees saw Jesus sitting with the people, they would consider the "lowlifes;" they said, "Why does your teacher eat with tax collectors and sinners?" Hearing this, Jesus said to them, "Those who are well have no need of a physician, but those who are sick. But go and learn what this means: 'I desire mercy and not sacrifice.' For I did not come to call the righteous, but sinners, to repentance" (Matthew 9:11–13).

Jesus didn't want robot friends. Jesus didn't want their sacrifice. Jesus wanted their hearts. Jesus didn't want their pity. Jesus didn't want their duty. Jesus came to save the lost, the sinners, and the ones who knew they needed a Savior. He was after the heart. He's still after the heart.

Beloved, Jesus desires relationship with you. Like the best friend you will ever have, He comes close and stays close. He wants to be invited into every part of your life, because He wants to give you an even better life. His heart for you is only good. ◊

DECLARATION *Prayer*

Jesus, You Are My Friend.
Thank You for sticking close no matter what season of life I'm walking through. Thank You for showing me what real friendship looks like and the heart of a real friend. I want to do life with You. I want You in my every moment of every day. Thank You for loving me and wanting a real relationship with me. You are the Friend that I need most. Jesus, You are everything.

JESUS
My Freedom

––––––

"Therefore if the Son makes you free, you shall be free indeed."

JOHN 8:36 NKJV

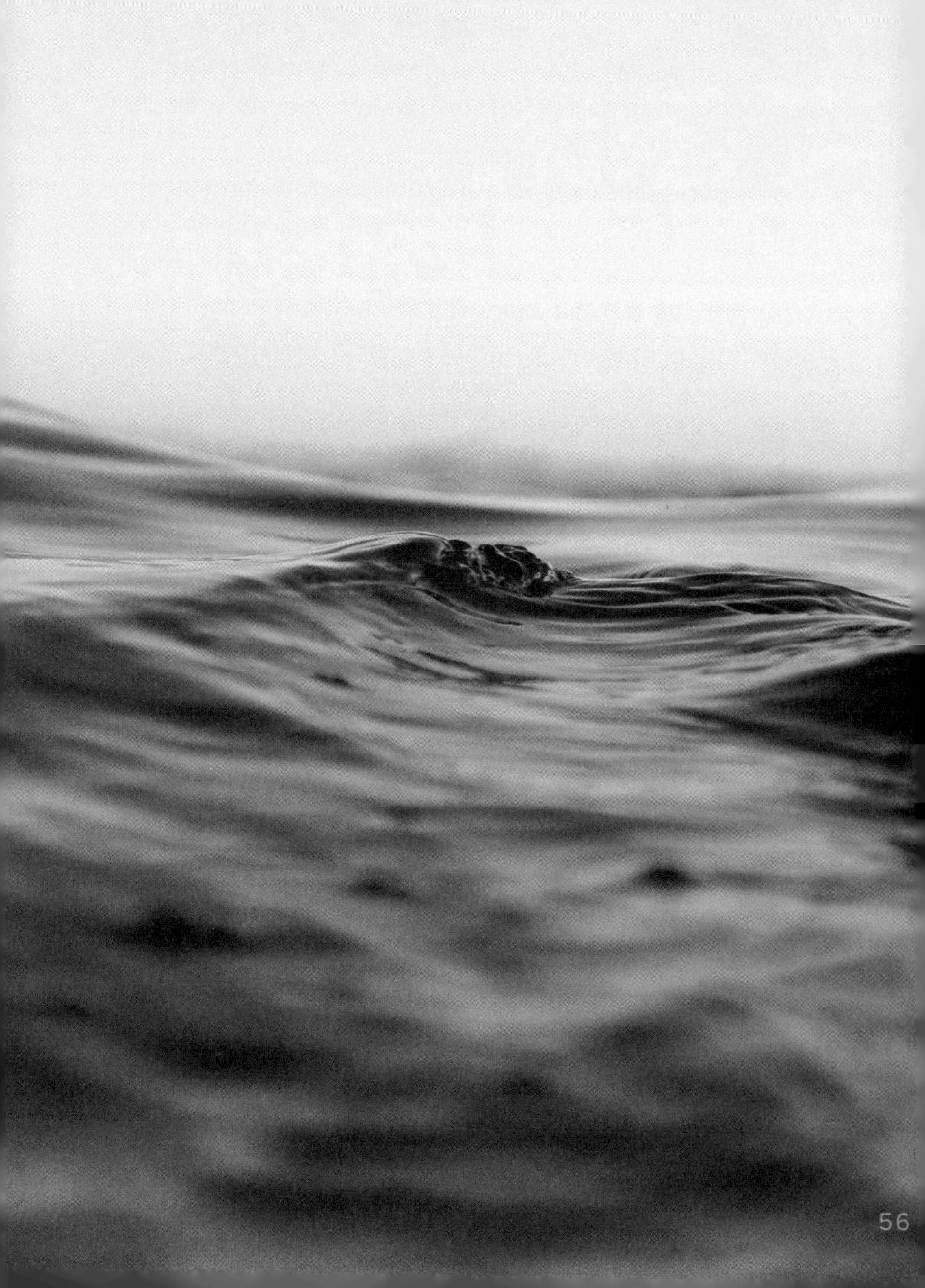

Jesus came to give us life and life more abundantly, but how can we live abundantly if we aren't walking in freedom? Did you know that the key to your freedom is as simple as receiving what is already yours?

The world tells us if we want something we must go out and get it, earn it, or achieve it, but with Jesus, things work opposite of the world. Everything you could ever need or want is in the Father's hand. The key to your freedom from addiction, depression, fear, and torment has already been given to you.

To set oneself free is impossible. The weight of sin is too heavy for any human to bare on their own, much less find their own way out. The good news is, Jesus already found the way out and He's inviting you to take His hand and let Him carry you out. You don't have to do it alone.

Over and over again we see in the Gospels that freedom was found in one moment and one encounter with Jesus. Look at the woman who was caught in adultery in John chapter eight. The woman was brought before Jesus because the religious leaders thought that He would shame her and reject her, but in that very moment she found the freedom she so desperately needed. With only eyes of love, true mercy, and extravagant grace, Jesus sets her free. Freedom happened through His love and acceptance. There was absolutely zero shame.

Do you know that even in your darkest moment, you are the most loved you will ever be? God's love and acceptance of you is not dependent on your performance. Jesus already decided long ago that He loved you and wanted you. Nothing you could ever do will change His mind about you, because the decision has already been made.

You have been chosen, loved, accepted, and forever freed. John 8:36 says, "Therefore if the Son makes you free, you shall be free indeed." So, son/daughter, be free as the Son has made you free indeed. ◊

Freedom happened through **JESUS'** *love and acceptance. There was absolutely zero shame.*

DECLARATION *Prayer*

Jesus, You Are My Freedom.
In Your eyes, I find extravagant love and grace. Thank You for loving me. Your love sets me free. I'm no longer a slave to sin or to the things of this world. I am a child of an all-loving Father who sees no spot in me. Thank You, Jesus, for this freedom that I freely receive from You. It is in Your name I pray. Thank You, Jesus!

JESUS
My Faith

---

*"And His name, through faith in His name,
has made this man strong, whom you
see and know. Yes, the faith which comes
through Him has given him this perfect
soundness in the presence of you all."*

ACTS 3:16 NKJV

In Acts chapter 3, we see a man healed who had been lame from birth. He was carried to the temple where he normally would beg for money. When Peter and John approached him, he reached out his hand expecting that they would give him money, but Peter said to him, "Silver and gold I do not have, but what I do have I give you: *In the name of Jesus Christ of Nazareth, rise up and walk*" (Acts 3:6, emphasis added). Immediately, the man stood to his feet. Walking, leaping, and praising God, the man entered the temple with Peter and John.

All the people that saw the man walking and praising God stood in awe and amazement, because they knew it was the man who was lame who had been begging at the gate of the temple. I love Peter's response after he sees that everyone is so amazed; he says,

> *"Men of Israel, why do you marvel at this? Or why look so intently at us,* as though by our own power or godliness we had made this man walk? The God of Abraham, Isaac, and Jacob, the God of our fathers, glorified His Servant Jesus, *whom you delivered up and denied in the presence of Pilate, when he was determined to let Him go. But you denied the Holy One and the Just, and asked for a murderer to be granted to you, and killed the Prince of life, whom God raised from the dead, of which we are witnesses.* And His name, through faith in His name, has made this man strong, whom you see and know. Yes, the faith which comes through Him has given him this perfect soundness in the

presence of you all "(Acts 3:12–16, emphasis added).

Notice the people marveled at the miracle that had happened, but Peter brought them back to who it was all about—Jesus. *Jesus* is the One who made the man who had been lame from the womb completely healed. *Jesus'* name is the name that brought the man to his feet! *Jesus* IS our faith! He is our reason to believe and the only One by which we are healed and set free! Also, notice that Peter makes it clear that it was not by their own power or godliness that they made the man walk! He knew it was not in his own strength and not of himself. Peter knew that it was all *Jesus*.

So, what part did Peter and John play in all of this? And what part can you and I play in our own walk of faith? Just *believe*. Believe in the name of Jesus and the One who was sent for your faith to be started and totally completed.

Hebrew 12:2 says, "looking unto Jesus, the author and finisher of *our* faith . . ."

So where do you find your faith? "Looking unto Jesus." Jesus is the One who makes your faith complete. Trying to muster up enough faith for your miracle can feel like an exhausting endless cycle of striving and earning; but when you look unto Jesus, you can recognize that your faith is already complete, lacking *nothing*. ◊

DECLARATION *Prayer*

Jesus, You Are My Faith.

I thank You that all I have to do is believe. You are the Author and the Finisher of my faith and because of You, I lack nothing. I put all my faith in who You are and in Your name that is above it all. I choose to look to You for everything that I will ever need. Thank you, Jesus!

JESUS
My Satisfaction

You open Your hand and satisfy
the desire of every living thing.

PSALM 145:16 NKJV

One of the biggest lies we believe as Christians is that anything other than Jesus can satisfy our souls. This lie is the oldest one in the book, yet somehow, we as humans continue falling for it. It started in the garden with Adam and Eve, when Satan told Eve to eat of the tree that God had said not to eat from. Satan convinced Eve that the fruit of this tree would surely satisfy her and that is why God didn't want her to have it (see Genesis 3). Does this lie sound familiar to you? Oh, how often we believe the lie that God doesn't want us to have something good; but how can that possibly be true when God is only good?

Satan will always lead you to believe that to satisfy the flesh is to be truly satisfied, but flesh does not satisfy the spirit, though the spirit can satisfy the flesh. Once we are in Jesus, we are no longer satisfied by flesh, but by the Spirit who gives life. Have you ever noticed that after coming to Jesus sin begins to lose its taste? Like suddenly sinning isn't fun anymore? Beloved, that is because your sinful and fleshly nature is no longer who you are.

Second Corinthians 5:17 says, "If anyone is in Christ, he is a NEW creation; old things have passed away; behold all things have become NEW" (emphasis added). You might be thinking, *If Jesus has made me new and truly satisfies my soul, why do I still crave things of the flesh?* This feeling is why many of us continue going back to the old things; but my next question for you would be this: Where are you looking? When you have the urge to turn back to the things of old, do you look to yourself (the flesh) to be your strength? Or, are you looking unto Jesus, the only One who can truly satisfy every desire?

Isaiah 55:2–3 says, "Why do you spend money for what is not bread, and your wages for what does not satisfy? Listen carefully to Me, and eat what is good, and let your soul delight itself in abundance. Incline your ear, and come to Me. Hear, and your soul shall live; and I will make an everlasting covenant with you . . ."

This is a prophecy from Isaiah about who was to come, Jesus. In this verse, he's not actually talking about bread you buy from the store, but about the Bread of Life. Jesus is good. Jesus is the abundance that we delight in that gives life to our souls. Jesus has made an everlasting promise to you that satisfies forever.

I've heard countless stories of men and women who, even in the midst of their sin, started speaking the name of Jesus over themselves. Day after day when fleshly desires would come, they would speak the name of Jesus and His gift of righteousness over themselves, sometimes while in the very act of sin. And day after day, the flesh got weaker and their spirit grew stronger. Sin began to lose its taste, and flesh completely lost its power. Jesus changes our desires to the point that He is the only One who can truly satisfy. ◊

DECLARATION *Prayer*

Jesus, You Are My Satisfaction.
You are the only One who can truly satisfy my soul and every need that I have. I look to You to satisfy me in every moment of every day. Guard my heart from the lies of the enemy that anything other than You could truly leave me satisfied. I thank You that I am no longer a slave to the flesh, but I'm a carrier of Your Spirit. I belong to You. Thank You, Jesus.

JESUS
My Victory

The sting of death is sin, and the strength of sin is the law. But thanks be to God, who gives us the victory through our Lord Jesus Christ.

1 CORINTHIANS 15:56–57 NKJV

Beloved, victory is yours. Through the blood of Jesus, you are forever victorious. The fight, the battle, the struggle, is over. You might have heard the saying, "We don't fight *for* victory, we fight *from* victory!" The reason we can live from a place of victory today is because of the price that was paid and the love that Jesus poured out for us on the cross. Our victory over sin is because Jesus faced every temptation that we face and yet He stood victorious over it all. Your victory over sin and every curse of the enemy is found in the blood of Jesus.

Maybe you're reading this right now and thinking, *I've heard all of this before, but I'm still not living a victorious life.*

There is powerful, life-changing truth in Scripture that we often overlook. First Corinthians 15:56 tells us that "the strength of sin is the law," but what does this mean? In Jesus, we have been redeemed from the law: "For the law was given through Moses, but grace and truth came through Jesus Christ" (John 1:17). As believers in Jesus, too often we live our lives as if Jesus never came, focusing on the law when the law is actually what gives sin its strength.

Do you ever feel in a moment of fight and struggle that all you can do is focus on the fight and the struggle? This, my friend, is the same as to focus on the law and sin. "But thanks *be* to God, who gives us the victory through our Lord Jesus Christ" (1 Corinthians 15:57). So where is our victory found? In Jesus. Where are we to look for victory? To Jesus. Who IS our victory? Jesus. It's so simple; yet somehow, we often make it so complicated. Friend, look unto Jesus. It is there that you will live victoriously. ◊

DECLARATION *Prayer*

Jesus, You Are My Victory.
Thank You for conquering sin, death, and every curse of the enemy so that I could live a victorious life. Thank You, Jesus, that the fight is over. I look to You, where my true victory is found. May I not be caught in the struggle but be captivated by who You are and all that You've done for me. In Jesus' name; Amen.

JESUS

My Trust

Trust in the LORD with all your heart, and lean not on your own understanding; in all your ways acknowledge Him, and He shall direct your paths.

PROVERBS 3:5–6 NKJV

J esus, our trust. In Him, we get understanding for every
area of life and find wisdom for the path He has ahead
of us. In Him, are all things that pertain to life and godliness (see 2 Peter 1:3), but are we actually looking to Him for
"all things"? So many things we do in life seem "normal"
simply because "that's what everyone does;" but is that the
life designed for us under Jesus? I believe our trust in Him
will dramatically change the way we live if we begin to learn
what it truly means to acknowledge Him.

By definition, "acknowledge" means, "to accept or admit
the existence or truth of." Many of us when reading that
would say that we do acknowledge Jesus in "all our ways" simply because we admit His existence and believe He is true.
But let me give you some questions to get yourself thinking:
When you get sick, do you acknowledge, admit and believe
the truth that Jesus died for your healing? Do you find rest
and trust knowing that He is an all-powerful and healing
God? Do you see your Savior's hands pierced for your healing? God can use human hands to bring about our healing
and the wisdom of doctors, but do you believe that more than
anything and anyone else, your true trust is found in Jesus?

To "trust" means, "to have firm belief in the reliability,
truth, ability, or strength of someone or something." Does
your trust in Jesus look like this in every area of your life,
not just in the "normal" and culturally acceptable things,
but in "all things"? In a moment of fear or lack, do you first
acknowledge Jesus as your Peace and your Provider? When

bad news comes your way, do you acknowledge that Jesus already had the final say for your life? Do you believe His Word to be true, over every negative word that is spoken over you? Do you acknowledge Jesus when you sin and the grace that He has lavished on you to be free from it?

No other person can give you the assurance and peace you so desperately long for. Paul said in Philippians 3:8, "Yet indeed I also count *all things* loss for the excellence of the knowledge of Christ Jesus my Lord, for whom I have suffered the loss of *all things*, and count them as rubbish, that I may gain Christ" (emphasis added).

"All things" are loss compared to the knowledge of Jesus Christ. May we know Him fully in all things and in every part of our lives. ◊

DECLARATION *Prayer*

Jesus, You Are My Trust.
What a life-changing truth it is to learn to acknowledge You in all things. Open my eyes Father to the areas of my life that You want to fill with the fullness of the cross. My trust is in You, Jesus. My life is Yours. Thank You for Your promises that will never fail me. In Jesus' name; Amen.

JESUS

My Qualification

---

*But God has chosen the foolish things
of the world to put to shame the wise,
and God has chosen the weak things of the
world to put to shame the things which are
mighty; and the base things of the world
and the things which are despised God
has chosen, and the things which are not,
to bring to nothing the things that are,
that no flesh should glory in His presence.*

1 CORINTHIANS 1:27–29 NKJV

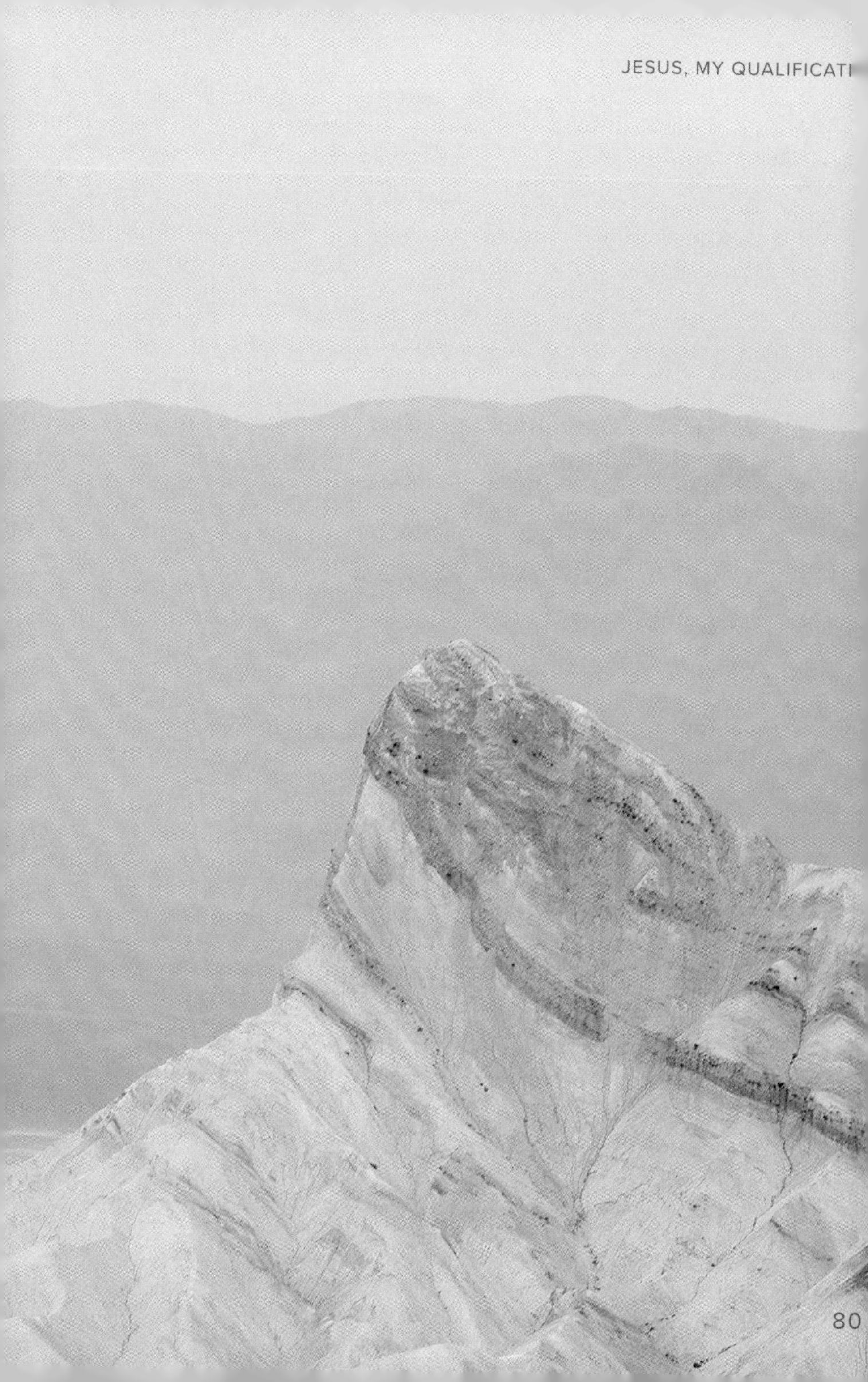

The Bible is full of stories of men and women who, by the world's standards, were not qualified for the thing they set out to do. Yet, God abundantly qualified them. In the world we live in, so often before we ask someone about who they are, we ask them what they do. This world is run by titles and status; but when we belong to Jesus, nothing can qualify us more than His blood. Jesus' blood not only makes you righteous, but His blood qualifies you for new levels of opportunity and favor that the world would otherwise say are impossible. You are no longer qualified by your own goodness, but by the goodness of Jesus.

Like most of us in moments, Moses got caught up with himself. In Exodus chapters three and four, we see God calling Moses to lead the Israelites out of Egypt, but the only thing stopping Moses was himself. Moses had trouble seeing past his own ability and weaknesses instead of realizing the One who was calling Him was also going to qualify him and be everything he needed to fulfill what God was leading him to do.

In Exodus 3:11 Moses said to God, "Who am I that I should go to Pharaoh, and that I should bring the children of Israel out of Egypt?"

Who am I? Do you ever feel like Moses did? Maybe Jesus is leading you to take a leap in your job or do something you've never done before and you've been asking this same question. Like Moses, maybe all you can see is you, your weakness, your inability. The beautiful thing is, what was true for Moses, is also true for you. Yes, you are weak. Yes, you are unqualified. Yes, you need help. In your own strength, what God is asking you to do is impossible; but just like God replied to Moses in Exodus, He also says to you, "I will certainly be with you" (3:12).

Your qualification for life is not found in yourself, your ability, the title that's been given to you, or all the things you've achieved in life. Jesus' blood has qualified you, and that's the best qualification you will ever have in this life. ◊

Not that we are sufficient of ourselves to think of anything as being from ourselves, but our sufficiency is from God.

2 CORINTHIANS 3:5

DECLARATION *Prayer*

Jesus, You Are My Qualification.
In You, I have everything I will ever need. I believe that You can do anything You want to do with my life. Help me to look to You as the One who qualifies me for every blessing and every opportunity. I believe You're leading me and going before me in every moment. Thank You for Your faithfulness. In Jesus' name; Amen.

JESUS

My Keeper

---

*You will keep him in perfect
peace, whose mind is stayed on
You, because he trusts in You.*

ISAIAH 26:3 NKJV

So often, we put so much pressure on ourselves to "keep" ourselves. We strive to keep ourselves pure, holy, innocent, and protected. This pressure we put on ourselves is not what God intended for us.

Everything in the Bible points to Jesus; we must remember that our faith, our belief, our trust, and our focus should never be on us.

You will never have enough willpower or determination to "keep" yourself. Willpower and determination are not what set you free. Jesus set you free; and because of this, HE is the only One who can "keep" you free.

Look at Isaiah 26:3, "You will keep *him* in perfect peace, whose mind is stayed *on You*, because he trusts in You." Notice it does not say, "the person will keep himself in perfect peace, whose mind is stayed on himself, because he trusts in himself." No, it says, "YOU" will keep in perfect peace, whose mind is stayed on "YOU," because he trusts in "YOU." Everything in His Word is pointing us to Jesus.

Look at Peter in Matthew 14:22–33. When Peter saw Jesus walking on the water, he called out to Him, "Lord if it's You, tell me to come to You on the water." After Peter said this, Jesus said to Him, "Come." Peter got out of the boat, walked on the water, and came toward Jesus, but when Peter saw the wind, he became afraid and began to sink. Notice, Peter didn't start sinking until he looked at the wind. The moment Peter took his eyes off Jesus was the moment he became afraid and started to sink.

This is the moment a lot of us have in common with Peter. We step out of the boat, we're walking on water, and then we take our eyes off Jesus. We see the wind of fear and the waves of our own weaknesses, and it is there we lose sight of our Keeper.

Psalm 121:7–8 says, "The LORD will keep you from all harm—he will watch over your life; the LORD will watch over your coming and going both now and forevermore" (NIV).

Friend, you have a Keeper, one who watches over your life and protects you from all harm. He promises to watch over your coming and going, both now and forevermore. You can trust Him; and the more you look to Him, the more you will see this to be true.

Romans 8:6 says, "The mind governed by the flesh is death, but the mind governed by the Spirit is life and peace" (NIV). Focusing on the flesh does not bring life to your spirit, but focusing on the Spirit, His Spirit in you, will bring life and peace. ◊

Jesus sets you free;
and because of this,
HE is the only One who
can "keep" you free.

DECLARATION *Prayer*

Jesus, You Are My Keeper.

I thank You that all the pressure to "keep" myself has been placed on You. I realize that I could never have enough willpower or determination to "keep" myself pure, holy, righteous, or protected. Thank You for Your promise to keep me and watch over my life now and forever. I look to You, and I trust You. Thank You, Jesus!

JESUS

My Kinsman Redeemer

He has sent redemption to His people;
He has commanded His covenant forever:
holy and awesome is His name.

PSALM 111:9 NKJV

Beloved, no matter who you are or where you've been, nothing is too big for your Redeemer. He came to save that which was lost and in need, and that, my friend, is you and me. Did you know that not only do you have a Redeemer, but you have a Kinsman Redeemer? Maybe you've never heard of a kinsman redeemer before, but today we're going to discover what this means by looking at the story of Ruth.

Although I feel like many people often focus on the determination of Ruth in this story, I want us to look at Boaz. Put yourself in the shoes of Ruth and see Jesus in the heart of Boaz. Boaz was Ruth's kinsman redeemer. Ruth didn't do anything to earn Boaz; by blood he was her kinsman. A "kinsman redeemer" is a relative in the position to redeem you out of your debt or your widowhood, or to avenge your debt. THIS is who Boaz was to Ruth, and this is who your Kinsman Redeemer Jesus is to you.

Jesus is your Kinsman Redeemer. Just like Boaz had to be related by blood to Ruth to redeem her, Jesus became a man, so that He could be blood-related to you to redeem you. Jesus wanted to be your Kinsman Redeemer. He wanted to pay your debt. He wanted and still longs to redeem you from loneliness, depression, and your past. He wants to defend, provide, heal, and deliver you.

In the story of Ruth, we see that Ruth gathered wheat in the fields that belonged to Boaz. When Boaz saw this, he then told his workers to purposefully drop grain for her and not rebuke her (see Ruth 2:16). Boaz was providing for Ruth and defending her even before she needed defending.

Just as Boaz told the workers to purposefully spill grain for Ruth to pick up, Jesus purposefully spilled His blood for you. In His blood is full redemption. Ephesians 1:7 says, "In Him we have redemption through His blood, the forgiveness of sins, according to the riches of His grace."

Friend, according to the riches of His grace, you have been redeemed. May you receive this redemption today through His blood, and rest in your Kinsman Redeemer. ◊

Jesus *purposefully spilled His blood for you. In His blood is full redemption.*

DECLARATION *Prayer*

Jesus, You Are My Kinsman Redeemer.
By the riches of Your grace, You have redeemed me. I thank You for becoming a man so that I could be blood-bought and blood-redeemed. Thank You for loving me so deeply. I receive my full redemption from You today. I no longer choose to look at the past, but I choose to look unto the cross where You did what I could not do for myself. Thank You Jesus; Amen.

JESUS

My Gracious Gift

---

*But the free gift is not like the offense.
For if by the one man's offense many died,
much more the grace of God and the gift
by the grace of the one Man, Jesus Christ,
abounded to many. And the gift is not like
that which came through the one who sinned.
For the judgment which came from one
offense resulted in condemnation, but the
free gift which came from many offenses
resulted in justification.*

ROMANS 5:15–16 NKJV

If you grew up in church, you probably have heard a message or two about living righteous and plenty of messages on the results of sin, but do you ever feel like you're the only one who missed the class on "how to" live righteous and "how to" not sin?

The Bible says, "The strength of sin is the law" (1 Corinthians 15:56), but so often we make a law out of living righteous instead of letting righteousness be a fruit of our heart transformation. Jesus loves the heart. The Bible says that men look at the outward appearance, but God looks at the heart (see 1 Samuel 16:7). As people, I believe we often do this unintentionally even in church. We look for people to change on the outside before there has been a heart change on the inside. So often, we make a law out of changing, instead of letting grace do what it does. The law never made anyone righteous, only Jesus can do that.

I love Romans 5:15–16 in *The Passion Translation*: "Now, there is no comparison between Adam's transgression and the gracious gift that we experience. *For the magnitude of the gift far outweighs the crime.* It's true that many died because of one man's transgression, but how much greater will God's grace and his gracious gift of acceptance overflow to many because of what one Man, Jesus, the Messiah, did for us! And this free-flowing gift imparts to us much more than what was given to us through the one who sinned. For because of one transgression [Adam's sin in the garden], we are all facing a death sentence with a verdict of "Guilty!" But this gracious gift leaves us free from our many failures and brings us into the perfect righteousness of God—acquitted with the words, 'Not guilty!'"

The reason you and I can stand as those "not guilty" is the same reason we are able to live a righteous life, free from the bondage of sin and death. The gracious gift that was given to us through Jesus is our strength and our way to righteousness. Your freedom from sin isn't birthed out of trying harder. The Pharisees thought they kept the Law; they focused on the Law, day and night. Yet when Jesus came, they completely missed His heart.

In Matthew 23:25–26, Jesus said to the Pharisees, "... You are like one who will only wipe clean the outside of a cup or bowl, leaving the inside filthy. You are foolish to ignore the greed and self-indulgence that live like germs within you. You are blind and deaf to your evil. Shouldn't the one who cleans the outside also be concerned with cleaning the inside? You need to have more than clean dishes; you need clean hearts!" (TPT).

Trying to live righteously by our own effort, without letting Jesus clean our hearts, is like trying to clean the outside of a house while the inside is still filthy. Jesus, and His gracious gift of GRACE, is what cleans our hearts and leads us to a life of righteousness and true freedom. Striving only leads to more striving but receiving the gracious gift of grace leads to life and life abundantly. Friend, all there is for you to do is receive from Him what He has already done for you. ◊

DECLARATION *Prayer*

Jesus, You Are My Gracious Gift.

I thank You that righteousness is not something I was meant to earn, but something I can only receive from You. Your grace is my freedom and redemption. I receive Your extravagantly gracious gift today and thank You that it is changing me from the inside out. Only by Your gift of grace am I washed and made clean. In Jesus' name; Amen.

JESUS
My Escape

"Because he has set his love upon Me, therefore I will deliver him; I will set him on high, because he has known My name. He shall call upon Me, and I will answer him; I will be with him in trouble; I will deliver him and honor him. With long life I will satisfy him, and show him My salvation."

PSALM 91:14–16 NKJV

Friend, did you know that in Jesus you always have an escape? No matter your situation, when you set your love upon Jesus and call on His name, He promises to answer and deliver you. So many times in life, it seems we are in need of an escape. Can you remember the last time you thought to yourself, *If only there was a way out?* Or maybe you're currently in a situation where you've been praying for a way out and an escape from a situation or a thought pattern that continues to lead to darkness?

Beloved, I have good news for you today. Although it may feel like you're on your own, He is with you. Jesus has already gone before you, providing a way out and an escape from every path that leads to destruction or death. Jesus is the way out. Jesus is the escape.

Look at the criminals who hung next to Jesus on the cross:

> Then one of the criminals who were hanged blasphemed Him, saying, "If You are the Christ, save Yourself and us." But the other, answering, rebuked him, saying, "Do you not even fear God, seeing you are under the same condemnation? And we indeed justly, for we receive the due reward of our deeds; but this Man has done nothing wrong." Then he said to Jesus, "Lord, remember me when You come into Your kingdom." And Jesus said to him, "Assuredly, I say to you, today you will be with Me in Paradise" (Luke 23:39–43).

For the criminals who hung next to Jesus, it seemed that they got what they deserved. The criminals on the cross were reaping the consequences for their actions, but when one called on the name of Jesus—everything changed.

Physically, it was impossible for the man who was once a criminal to escape. There was nothing he could do in his own strength or willpower to save himself. He needed an escape and only Jesus could be what he needed.

By calling on Jesus, the criminal was set free from eternal death and completely forgiven. He didn't hop off the cross and find his own way out; no, Jesus was his only hope. And Jesus is *our* only hope.

Friend, your escape is as simple as the criminal who hung next to Jesus on the cross. Your way out is as simple as calling on His name. Jesus will be with you. He will rescue you. And He will be your escape from every form of darkness. ◊

_____

And Jesus *said to him, "Assuredly, I say to you, today you will be with Me in Paradise"*

LUKE 23:43

DECLARATION *Prayer*

Jesus, You Are My Escape.
Thank You for always making a way where there seems to be no way. Nothing is stronger than Your name and no situation is too difficult for You. No matter where I am, I know that I can call on Your name and You will deliver and rescue me. You will set me on high and You will be with me in trouble. I thank You, Jesus, that I never go anywhere alone. In Jesus' name; Amen.

My Completion

---

*And you are complete in Him, who is
the head of all principality and power.*

COLOSSIANS 2:10 NKJV

When you believe in Jesus, you can rest in knowing that He has made you complete. Though you were once lacking and in need of many things, Jesus came, fulfilled, and completed all that you were missing. If it is true that we have been made complete in Him, why are so many in lack? You might say that it is because we still live in this world, but Jesus said, "In the world you will have tribulation; but be of good cheer, I have overcome the world" (John 16:33).

If Jesus has defeated the world, and "as He is, so are we in this world" (1 John 4:17), then why is the "world" often our reason for defeat? Why are we making excuses and allowances for a life that is less than what was designed for us and made possible through Jesus?

Colossians 2:8–10 says, "Beware lest anyone cheat you through philosophy and empty deceit, according to the tradition of men, according to the basic principles of the world, and not according to Christ. For in Him dwells all the fullness of the Godhead bodily; and you are complete in Him, who is the head of all principality and power."

So often even as believers, we settle for a less-than life because we give into the empty deceit and philosophy according "to the tradition of men." We must know that the "basic principles" of this world, are often not in line with truth.

The traditions of men tell us that we must earn and strive for our provision for life; but His Word says, "And my God shall supply all your need according to His riches in glory by Christ Jesus" (Philippians 4:19). The traditions of men tell us that we must look to ourselves to prove and qualify for blessings and favor, but His Word says that He has already qualified us for every blessing (see Colossians 1:12, Ephesians 1:3). The traditions of men tell us to put our trust in men, but His Word says to trust in HIM with all our heart and He will direct our steps (see Proverbs 3:5).

There are so many different traditions that have become so normal, even to believers; but these traditions are not based on truth and were never meant to be our guide and source of life. The traditions of men are not where we will find the life we are looking for; only Jesus can give us true everlasting life.

Colossians 2:6 says, "As you therefore have received Christ Jesus the Lord, so walk in Him." So how do we live a life that is complete in Jesus? As we received Him, so we walk in Him. And how did we receive Him? Only by faith. To walk complete is to walk with faith in Jesus. Faith does not come from this world but by hearing, and hearing by the Word of God (see Romans 10:17).

If you are in need or lacking anything today, tune your ears to hear what He is saying to you. His words will bring you faith to walk out this life fully complete in Him. ◊

DECLARATION *Prayer*

Jesus, You Are My Completion.
In You, I believe I have everything I will ever need. You are my truth and where my true help comes from. Help me to recognize the philosophies and traditions of men that I have allowed to take the place of faith in my life. Nothing can satisfy, fill, heal, or complete me like You can. Show me what it means to live my life complete, hidden in who You are. In Jesus' name; Amen.

My Healer

But He was wounded for our transgressions, He was bruised for our iniquities; the chastisement for our peace was upon Him, and by His stripes we are healed.

ISAIAH 53:5 NKJV

You might've heard, read, or recited this verse more times than you can count, but do you realize the power of what it truly means for you? Beloved, you have a Healer in the name of Jesus. The cross was not just for you to have forgiveness of your sins, but for you to experience resurrection life. In Jesus, you are redeemed from every curse of the enemy and all its fruit. Jesus came that you would have life and life more abundantly (see John 10:10). His desire for you is to be healthy and whole. I'll say that again . . . His desire is for you is to be healthy and WHOLE.

Jesus said in John 14:9, "He who has seen Me has seen the Father."

So how can we know that it is His desire that we are healed, healthy, and whole? We look at Jesus. Have you ever noticed that Jesus never passed up a sick person? When Jesus was walking the earth, we constantly see Him healing those with blind eyes, and telling the lame to walk. If Jesus' heart wasn't for us to be made well, then Jesus would not have healed the sick and the lame.

Proverbs 4:22 says that His Word is "life to those who find them, and health to all their flesh." It's so important to meditate on His Word. There are so many voices in this world that speak the opposite of truth. Oftentimes, even our bodies say otherwise.

But there is a name that is stronger than the diagnosis you've been given. His Word says that God exalted Jesus to the highest place, giving Him the name that is above every name that is to be named. In Jesus, you hold the name that is more powerful than sickness of every kind.

If you need healing, I'm here to remind you that the Lover of your heart, body, and soul desires for you to be well. It is not God's will that anyone should perish, but that all would have eternal life. Eternal life starts now. Life abundantly and whole.

Don't believe the lie that you are supposed to be sick. Don't accept the curse of sin and death when Jesus paid for you to have LIFE. His stripes hold your healing, and with each lash He was thinking of you. ◊

I [Jesus] *have come that they may have life, and that they may have it more abundantly.*

JOHN 10:10

DECLARATION *Prayer*

Jesus, You Are My Healer.
Thank You for giving Your life so that I could experience resurrection life. You have healed, redeemed, and freed me from every work of the enemy. I receive all that You died to give me, and by Your stripes I am healed and made whole. Thank You, Jesus!

LANEY RENE

JESUS

My Righteousness

———————

*For if by the one man's offense death
reigned through the one, much more those
who receive abundance of grace and of
the gift of righteousness will reign in life
through the One, Jesus Christ.*

ROMANS 5:17 NKJV

Have you ever thought, *If only I could be the person I used to be?* Do you ever find yourself measuring your worth by your own efforts? One day you are close to God, but the next you are far away, all based on your own ability to draw near. This way of thinking is an endless cycle and is unfortunately common in many church settings and Bible studies. So often, we spend our days focused on our own goodness and trying to earn our own righteousness when true righteousness cannot be earned.

When someone gives you a gift, you would never respond by asking, "How much do I owe you?" A gift is just that—something given freely without payment.

Trying to earn righteousness is like trying to pay Jesus back for a gift we could truly never afford. It's like saying the price Jesus paid wasn't enough; but what a difference it makes when we learn to receive the gift. In one moment, all our focus turns from ourselves to the beauty and wonder of Jesus. Self-effort draws attention to self but receiving the free gift of righteousness will make others stand in awe of who He is.

The day you accepted Jesus, you accepted His righteousness for you. Nothing you could ever do will take away this gift. Your righteousness is not based on how much you serve, give, or sacrifice. The sacrifice has already been made. Your righteousness is based on what Jesus has already done, and that will never be taken away from you. You are not your past mistakes, and you are not your greatest successes.

These things are both like filthy rags in comparison to the righteousness of Jesus. So, don't waste your efforts in trying to reach something you can never achieve on your own. Just receive from where there is an abundance. Jesus is your forever righteousness. ◊

DECLARATION *Prayer*

Jesus, You Are My Righteousness.
Thank You for paying the price that I could never pay on my own. Thank You for taking on all my sin and unrighteousness so I could freely receive Your righteousness. I don't want to strive to achieve my worth from the praises of others. I want to rest and live from the righteousness that You have already freely given me. May Your gift of righteousness be my identity and where I live from each day. It is in Your name I pray. Thank You, Jesus!

JESUS
My Sound Mind

———————

*And do not be conformed to this world,
but be transformed by the renewing of your
mind, that you may prove what is that good
and acceptable and perfect will of God.*

ROMANS 12:2 NKJV

God has given us a sound mind, but what exactly is a "sound mind"? I think many of us may hear the words "sound mind" and think, *I just want to turn the sound off!* Our minds, though they don't have a mouth, never stop talking to us. We have thousands of different thoughts every day, which means we get thousands of different opportunities to dwell on life or death. Though often it may feel like our minds have authority over us and we don't get to choose what we think, it's important to remember one of the many things we've been given through Jesus is a sound mind.

A sound mind is a fruit of the renewal of our minds. And the renewal of our minds comes from setting our minds on the beauty of Jesus and all that He has done for us. Romans 12:2 says, "And do not be conformed to this world, but be transformed by the renewing of your mind, that you may prove what is that good and acceptable and perfect will of God."

Being "conformed to this world" is letting the world control your mind and have power over your thoughts. The thoughts produced by this world are the ones that don't line up with the truth in His Word. The world's thoughts are death to your soul, but the Word of God is life to those who find it and health to all their flesh (see Proverbs 4:22). The Word of God is health to your mind!

Philippians 4:8-9 says, "Finally, brethren, whatever things are true, whatever things are noble, whatever things are just, whatever things are pure, whatever things are lovely, whatever things are of good report, if *there is* any virtue and if *there is* anything praiseworthy—meditate on these things. The things which you learned and received and heard and saw in me, these do, and the God of peace will be with you."

To meditate on things that are true, noble, just, pure, lovely, of good report, and praiseworthy will bring peace to your heart and mind. God has given you authority over your mind. And you get to choose what you dwell on. There is so much power in what you believe and every belief system you have starts with one thought.

Have you ever noticed how you can hear of someone else dealing with a certain condition, whether it be a sickness or a circumstance, and you can immediately start thinking you have the same exact problem? It could be something as simple as ant stings and suddenly you start feeling incredibly itchy! This, my friend, is the power of your mind. The power of dwelling and meditating on things can actually change your reality.

So first, remember what you have been given—a sound mind. Meditate on His love for you and the gift that has already been given to you. Take back what is already yours; exercise authority over your thoughts: "For the weapons of our warfare are not carnal but mighty in God for pulling down strongholds, casting down arguments and every high thing that exalts itself against the knowledge of God, bringing every thought into captivity to the obedience of Christ" (2 Corinthians 10:4–5). ◊

DECLARATION *Prayer*

Jesus, You Are My Sound Mind.
When I think on all You have done for me, my mind begins to change and be filled with peace. I know You have given me power and authority over every thought that rises up against Your name. I speak Your name over my mind, over my body, and over my soul. Jesus, captivate me with who You are and renew me from the inside out. In Jesus' name; Amen.

JESUS

My Good Father

"I and My Father are one."

JOHN 10:30 NKJV

J esus is our good Father. He came to reveal the Father's heart to us, and by looking at Him we can know our Father's heart toward us is only good. You may have grown up without a father, or with a father who hinders you from understanding what a good father is like. Or maybe you had an incredible father. But the truth is—no earthly father, whether good or bad, compares to our Heavenly Father.

He is a close Papa and a Friend; the Papa who named you and claimed you. He is the Papa who holds you and frees you. He is always gracious and kind, always looking to heal, redeem, restore, and affirm you. He calls you His own, and is never ashamed or embarrassed of you. He stands and shouts, "He/She is mine!" in every moment. His pride in calling you His own is not dependent on your performance, but in who you are as "HIS" child. Nothing can stop His love for you, and nothing you do could ever make Him prouder of you.

The heart of the Father is seen so clearly in Jesus because Jesus and the Father are one. Jesus only did what He first saw His Father doing. Because of Jesus, we know that the heart of the Father is love in its fullest expression, "Greater love has no one than this, than to lay down one's life for his friends" (John 15:13). The Father, through Jesus, laid down His life for us. His extravagant love is what brought Him to us and keeps Him coming after us. Love is what brought Him to the cross and love is what brought Him back to life. He did it all out of His extravagant love for us. Is this the Papa you know? Did you know this is the heart of your Father?

One of the most popular verses in the Bible starts with the words, "For God so loved . . ." (John 3:16). He loved us so much that He sent His one and only Son to die for us. So often, we make the narrative of the story about us finding Jesus, but we must realize we would've never found Him unless He had come after us. The real story will always start with the Father's love coming after the ones He couldn't live without.

First John 3:1 says, "Behold, what manner of love the Father has bestowed on us, that we should be called children of God! . . ." The word "bestow" means "to present as a gift." The love that the Father has for you is given; it's a gift. His love is not earned or achieved or paid back. It is simply an extravagant gift from an extravagant Father. His love is the sweetest and best gift you could ever receive.

Matthew 7:11 says, "If you then, being evil, know how to give good gifts to your children, how much more will your Father who is in heaven give good things to those who ask Him!" Take note of the words here, "how much more." Beloved, there is more, more of Him to behold, to discover, to experience, and to enjoy. Psalm 145:3 says, ". . . For there is no end to the discovery of the greatness that surrounds you" (TPT).

If you feel lonely, there is more of Him to discover, for your Father is a "God of all comfort" (see 2 Corinthians 1:3–5). If you are in need, there is more of Him to experience; for your Father provides for all your needs (see Philippians 4:19). If you are brokenhearted, there is more of Him to behold; for your Father is a Healer and near to the brokenhearted (see Psalm 34:18). If you're in want, there is more of Him to enjoy; for your Father satisfies the desire of every living thing (see Psalm 145:16).

This is the truth about your Father. Jesus said, "If you had known Me, you would have known My Father also; and from now on you know Him and have seen Him" (John 14:7). If you want to know more of your Father's heart, just look at Jesus. Jesus reveals the Father's heart to us. ◊

DECLARATION *Prayer*

Jesus, You Are My Good Father.
Thank You for Your gift of love that You have bestowed upon me. I want to discover "the more" of who You are. If my view of who You are as Father is broken, heal my heart and show me who You really are. Help me to see Your goodness and love through Jesus and experience You as my close Papa. You comfort me, restore me, heal me, redeem me, and fill me with life. You're better than I ever imagined. Thank You, Father.

JESUS

My Health

———————

*Beloved, I pray that you may
prosper in all things and be in health,
just as your soul prospers.*

3 JOHN 1:2 NKJV

When you hear the word "health," what is the first thing that comes to your mind? Maybe it's the current state of your body's health, your mental health, or the health of the relationships in your life; but did you know that your gift of health is not limited? The health that Jesus has for you is for your whole being—mind, body, and soul.

The amazing thing about Jesus, is that many times when we receive His health for one area of our life, it affects all the others. The health of Jesus is not partial, but it's given to you total and complete. When we begin to receive the health He has for us in our soul, our soul will then begin to affect our mind. And when we receive His health for our mind, our mind will then affect our body. The health of Jesus is contagious, giving life to every part of us. 1 Corinthians 6:20 says, "For you were bought at a price; therefore glorify God in your body and in your spirit, which are God's."

". . . therefore glorify God in your body and in your spirit." *To glorify* means to "praise, celebrate, and magnify." Doesn't this bring a whole new perspective to what it means to glorify God in our body and spirit? So often, instead of praising, celebrating, and magnifying Jesus, we tend to magnify the problem, the symptom, or our current circumstance. We give praise, celebrate, and magnify things by what comes out of our mouth and also what we let live in our thoughts. Is there an area of your life that you're not experiencing the health of Jesus? Maybe take a minute and think about what it is you've been glorifying. Are you glorifying Jesus, the cross, and His resurrection? Or are you glorifying doubt, sickness, insecurity, or fear?

You have the power in Jesus' name to speak life and health into your body. You glorify God in your body and spirit when you glorify the death and resurrection of Jesus. The price you were bought with that Paul is talking about in 1 Corinthians 6:20 is the spotless blood of Jesus. His blood is what washes you from all unrighteousness and redeems you from every curse of the enemy. His blood is what bought you total health—mind, body, and soul. ◊

"Nevertheless, I will bring health and healing to it; I will heal my people and will let them enjoy abundant peace and security."

JEREMIAH 33:6 NIV

DECLARATION *Prayer*

Jesus, You Are My Health.

I speak Your name over my mind, body, and soul. You are the Light that gives life to my whole being. Today, I choose to glorify Your name instead of the works of the enemy. I believe in the fullness of the resurrection life that was paid for on my behalf. Jesus may You be glorified, praised, celebrated, and magnified in every part of me. In Jesus' name; Amen.

JESUS
My Finisher

---

*So when Jesus had received
the sour wine, He said, "It is
finished!" And bowing His head,
He gave up His spirit.*

JOHN 19:30 NKJV

As believers in Jesus, we know that Jesus sacrificed His life for us. We know that He paid the price that we could not pay for our sins and that He died a death we couldn't bear; but do you know the fullness of the redemption that came through His sacrifice? Many of us as believers in Jesus still don't know what we have truly been given. We may never fully know because there is always more of Him to discover, but that is the wonderful gift of the Christian life. Life with Jesus is a constant discovery of who He is and all that He has done for us.

John 19:28–30 says, "After this, Jesus, knowing that all things were now accomplished, that the Scripture might be fulfilled, said, 'I thirst!' Now a vessel full of sour wine was sitting there; and they filled a sponge with sour wine, put it on hyssop, and put it to His mouth. So when Jesus had received the sour wine, He said, 'It is finished!' And bowing His head, He gave up His spirit."

If Jesus cried out, "It is finished!," knowing that "all things were now accomplished," don't you want to know what all was accomplished and finished for you?

Often, it feels like this life can be all about accomplishing and finishing; we finish one thing only to start another. But what if the overwhelming pressure, the anxiousness for tomorrow, and the doubt of the end result was something you never had to think about again? When Jesus said, "It is finished," the "It" here holds more power than we can begin to imagine. That "It" is everything Jesus spoke, everything

He did, everything He prayed, everything He accomplished, and everything He finished. "IT" was finished for you.

So long, fear. So long, doubt. So long, insecurity. So long, depression. So long, sickness. So long, anxiety. So long to the past. So long, shame. So long, guilt. So long . . . because IT was finished.

Jesus paid the price that we could not pay and the sacrifice He made was not just for salvation, but for "It" to be finished in your life. What is the "It" that has been holding you back lately? What has been consuming your mind and stealing your peace and joy? Friend, it was finished, and Jesus is now the only One who holds power and authority over your mind.

Therefore, if anyone is in Christ, he is a new creation; old things have passed away, behold ALL THINGS have become new (2 Corinthians 5:17, emphasis added).

Friend, all things have been accomplished for you and all things have been made new. You are no longer a slave to the past, but a child of God and heir of all that was finished. ◊

DECLARATION *Prayer*

Jesus, You Are My Finisher.

There is no end to Your grace and what You've done for me. Thank You for accomplishing "all things" for me. Open up my eyes to see more of the "It" that You have finished in my life. I want to experience all that You are and all that You've finished for me. Thank you. In Jesus' name; Amen.

JESUS

My Acceptance

But God, who is rich in mercy, because of His great love with which He loved us, even when we were dead in trespasses, made us alive together with Christ (by grace you have been saved), and raised us up together, and made us sit together in the heavenly places in Christ Jesus.

EPHESIANS 2:4–6 NKJV

When we are kids, our desire for acceptance is obvious. Most kids will do anything for attention. We're born with a desire for acceptance and approval. As we get older, although that desire may not be as noticeable in the way we express it, that desire to be loved, seen, and accepted is 100% still there.

This desire for acceptance is a gift from God. Although this desire is one of the things the enemy tries to turn and use for harm in our life, the desire to be accepted is a gift if we allow it to draw us closer to the One who always accepts us.

The reason acceptance is often used for harm is because we think what we need is acceptance from other people. This striving to be accepted by people frequently leads to more striving and rejection. Although it's hard to accept, not everyone will accept you, understand you, or even love you. Look at Jesus! He IS perfect love and perfect in every way, yet people still do not accept Him, understand Him, or love Him.

The desire to be accepted is what will draw us to the only One who can truly accept us and love us for who we are. Jesus exemplified perfectly what acceptance is through His extravagant love and grace.

This world often says, "Do *this*, and then you will be accepted," but Jesus accepts you and loves you just as you are right now. Jesus came to the world because He "so loved the world" (see John 3:16), yet the world had done nothing for Him. The acceptance Jesus has for you is not based on performance. That is why the desire for His acceptance is liberating, leading you to more and more freedom.

Have you ever noticed the type of people Jesus attracted? He attracted the sinners, the tax collectors, and the ones who persecuted Christians. How can someone so perfect make those who are so far from perfection feel so wanted and accepted? Because true acceptance isn't based on performance, but on position.

> *But God still loved us with such great love. He is so rich in compassion and mercy. Even when we were dead and doomed in our many sins, he united us into the very life of Christ and saved us by his wonderful grace! He raised us up with Christ the exalted One, and we ascended with him into the glorious perfection and authority of the heavenly realm, for we are now co-seated as one with Christ!* (Ephesians 2:4–6 TPT).

Friend, you have been seated with Jesus in heavenly places. Because of the love and acceptance of Jesus, your position will never change. You are no longer positioned by *your* performance, but by *His* performance on the cross. You have forever been accepted by Jesus, and His love for you has no bounds. ◊

Jesus *accepts and loves*
you just as you are right now.

DECLARATION *Prayer*

Jesus, You Are My Acceptance.
Thank You for loving me before I could ever do a thing to earn your love. Thank You for the richness of Your mercy that covers every part of me. I rest in Your love and Your acceptance today. Thank You, Jesus!

My Worth

But God demonstrates His own love toward us, in that while we were still sinners, Christ died for us.

ROMANS 5:8 NKJV

No matter who we are or where we've come from, we all have a desire to know our worth. Whether it's knowing we're worth something to another person, or knowing that our life is worth living, there's a desire there to know we are worthy.

In our world and because of our culture today, we're very aware of the worth of money, but money is not the only thing that measures value.

Value is not strictly based on money, but worth is truly defined by what someone is willing to pay. Many things that cost a lot of money are not actually "worth" that much, but yet we still will pay it because of how much we value that thing personally.

This a beautiful picture of Jesus' love for you. Romans 5:8 says, ". . . while we were STILL sinners, Christ died for us." This means that in the midst of our unrighteousness and worthlessness, Jesus counted you and I worth His own life.

He counted us worthy of every lash on His back, the crown of thorns on His head, every nail that was pressed into His bones, and the piercing spear in His side. He wasn't only willing, but He longed to do the will of the Father, which was to die for us, so that we might live in Him. The depth in which He values us personally, we can't even begin to fathom.

Friend, your worth is not measured or defined by this world or the people in it. Your worth was forever solidified in the blood of Jesus. He called you worthy before you took a single breath. He called you worthy of life and worthy of His life. Nothing can add or take away this worth that He has already placed upon you.

You are worth it. Every moment, every day, every hour, you're worth His time, His patience, His love, His affection, His death, and His life. ◊

"Look at all the birds—do you think
they worry about their existence?
They don't plant or reap or store up
food, yet your heavenly Father
provides them each with food.
Aren't you much more valuable
to your Father than they?"

MATTHEW 6:26 TPT

DECLARATION *Prayer*

Jesus, You Are My Worth.
Nothing can define me more accurately than Your love. I find myself when I look into Your eyes of love. You have covered me with Your blood and now I'm forever made worthy. Thank You, Jesus, for paying the price for my life and my freedom. In Jesus' name; Amen.

JESUS
My Peace

Her ways are ways of pleasantness,
and all her paths are peace.

PROVERBS 3:17 ESV

Peace is such an interesting thing. Oftentimes, peace is hard to explain. One of the easiest ways to recognize peace is by recognizing what it feels like to be without it. Can you remember a season or situation when you didn't have peace? Or, maybe you're currently in a situation when you lack peace.

Friend, peace is a fruit of His Spirit. Peace is something that has been freely given to you by Jesus and through Jesus. Peace is yours for the taking.

Maybe you're thinking right now, *But if Jesus has truly given me peace, why am I not experiencing peace?* Good question. Although peace has been given to us by His Spirit, and it is ours for the taking, we also get to decide whether or not to receive it. Just like God gave us free will and free choice with everything else, He gives us a choice when it comes to following His peace.

When you become a child of God, the things of the flesh no longer satisfy you, but only the things of His Spirit. John 6:63 says, "It is the Spirit who gives life; the flesh profits nothing. . . ." Oftentimes, we can trace back to the moment our peace went missing, to that moment when we tried to satisfy the flesh instead of letting the Spirit satisfy us. Jesus didn't leave us, but the absence of His peace is simply because we chose to satisfy the flesh which is no longer satisfying, and no longer who we are anymore. Satisfying the flesh no longer truly satisfies, because we are now made of His Spirit.

This is not Jesus being cruel. He is not taking away the gift

He gave us. When we lack peace in our decisions, it's because we tried to mix death with life, and His peace is only life.

Life is full of decisions. Constantly we're answering the question, "This or that?" One of the simplest things I have learned that I can lean on in every situation is His peace. We can way overcomplicate things, but it's important to remember that God is not the author of confusion, but of peace (see 1 Corinthians 14:33). Following Jesus isn't complicated or confusing, but full of pleasantness and peace. Following Jesus is full of the fruit of His Spirit.

Friend, where do you need peace today? Where is it that you need to experience the presence of His Spirit that brings life? The good news—peace is already yours; all you have to do is receive it. Choose Jesus, who brings your spirit and true self life and peace. ◊

Peace is something that has been freely given to you by Jesus *and through* Jesus. *Peace is yours for the taking.*

DECLARATION *Prayer*

Jesus, You Are My Peace.

Your Spirit has given me life and now all that brings me true life is found in Your Spirit. I want to live in Your ways of pleasantness and follow Your paths of peace. I receive all that You died to give me. You have given me peace for my mind, body, and soul and I receive it all. Thank You, Jesus!

LANEY RENE

My Perfect Love

There is no fear in love;
but perfect love casts out fear,
because fear involves torment.
But he who fears has not
been made perfect in love.

1 JOHN 4:18 NKJV

Loneliness is one of our heart's greatest pains. To feel alone is often to feel forgotten, unwanted, and unseen. God created us with a desire for relationship. We don't have to look very far to see that He longs to fulfill that desire.

In Genesis 2, we see that God created Adam but Adam needed a companion. So God caused Adam to fall into a deep sleep and He created a companion for Adam named "Eve" out of one of Adam's own ribs. Adam and Eve were in the garden of Eden together when Eve still went looking for something more. God told them they could eat of any tree in the garden except for one, yet that was the one Satan deceived Eve into tasting.

Have you ever found yourself in a similar position? As though God says to you, "All that I have is yours," but you find yourself wondering what else might be out there that would satisfy? We often do this in relationships. Since no one is perfect, we can go through people like a bag of chips thinking that someone out there will one day satisfy all our desires. This, my friend, is one of the sneakiest of lies, and couldn't be further from the truth.

Whether it's a friend, family member, or spouse, there is only one Person who is meant to satisfy all your heart's desire. The longing that was there in Eve, is the same longing that we deal with today. Whether we're surrounded by an innumerable amount of friends, or have an incredible family life and marriage, only Jesus can meet our every need.

1 John 4:8 tells us that "God is love," which means without

God there is no love at all.

God's love is the only perfect love. His love swallows up our loneliness and fulfills every longing of our heart.

Psalm 68:6 says,

> *To the fatherless he is a father.*
> *To the widow he is a champion friend.*
> *To the lonely he makes them part of a family.*
> *To the prisoners he leads into prosperity until they sing for joy.*
> *This is our Holy God in his Holy Place!*
> *But for the rebels there is heartache and despair* (TPT).

Beloved, Jesus is your Father, your champion Friend, and you are a part of His family. No one and nothing else could ever give you more purpose, confidence, security, or comfort. ◊

DECLARATION *Prayer*

Jesus, You Are My Perfect Love.

Nothing and no one else can satisfy me like You do. You have loved me with a love that I will spend the rest of my life discovering. There is no end to all that You are to me. You are my comfort and Your presence has forever delivered me from loneliness. Loneliness is only a lie that has told me You're not with me, but I know that You are near. I rest in Your love and closeness to my heart. You are everything to me. In Jesus' name; Amen.

JESUS

My Rock

---

*"And I also say to you that you are
Peter, and on this rock I will build
My church, and the gates of Hades
shall not prevail against it."*

MATTHEW 16:18 NKJV

Do you ever feel like everything in your life is shaky? Like nothing is sure and everything could fall through the cracks at any given time? This way of life and thinking may be popular in the culture around us, but it's not the life that we were created to live.

Many times, Jesus is referred to as our "rock" in the Bible. Verses like Psalm 18:2, "The LORD is my rock and my fortress and my deliverer; my God, my strength, in whom I will trust," give us the picture of God being our firm foundation, but what makes this foundation strong enough for the church? Or, what makes this foundation strong enough to build our lives on?

Jesus told Peter in Matthew 16:18 that "on this rock I will build My church, and the gates of Hades [death] shall not prevail against it." Many of us might already know that the name *Peter* means "rock."

This foundation, this "rock" that Jesus told us to build the church on was Himself. So when we say, "Jesus is our rock and our firm foundation" (see 1 Corinthians 3:11; Matthew 7:24-27), He actually IS our rock and firm foundation. This is a metaphor, but still true. Jesus is our Rock, and this Rock is stronger than the wages of death.

Jesus went on to say in Matthew 16:19, "And I will give you the keys of the kingdom of heaven, and whatever you bind on earth will be bound in heaven, and whatever you loose on earth will be loosed in heaven."

If the keys of the kingdom have been given to us, then it

is time we unlock the kingdom in our world and the world around us. It is time to unlock the kingdom of the Rock. It is time we unlock the kingdom of life that reigns and triumphs over death. The kingdom is not one-half death and one-half life, but the kingdom is a foundation of freedom, life, grace, and love. The kingdom is a firm foundation.

Just before Jesus changed Peter's name from Simon to Peter, Jesus had asked His disciples a question. He asked, "Who do you say that I am?" And Peter responded, "You are the Christ, the Son of the living God." I love Peter's response here, because it put Jesus in His rightful place, acknowledging the power and authority of who He is.

Friend, instead of dwelling on death, shortcomings, and failures, put Jesus in His rightful place in your life; acknowledge His power and authority.

Psalm 40:2 says, "He also brought me up out of a horrible pit, out of the miry clay, and set my feet upon a rock, and established my steps."

This is who Jesus is to you. He will pull you out of a horrible pit and set your feet upon a rock. ◊

DECLARATION *Prayer*

Jesus, You Are My Rock.

You are my firm foundation and the One I build my life upon. You have rescued and redeemed me, pulled me out of the miry clay; and today, I acknowledge Your power and Your authority in my life. I acknowledge the gift of living in Your kingdom as one of Your own. I will not live afraid of calamity, for You are holding me up. Thank you, Jesus!

JESUS
My Favor

———————

*For You, O Lᴏʀᴅ, will bless the
righteous; with favor You will
surround him as with a shield.*

PSALM 5:12 NKJV

F riend, because of Jesus and His righteousness you received as a gift, you are surrounded with favor. This favor is not something you have to earn, but it was given to you as a gift when you became a child of God.

Unlike the favor of man, God's favor does not come and go. His favor is not something you can earn or lose. His favor is placed upon you like a crown of grace. You have the favor of God's perfect Son, Jesus, who deserves all blessings and favor. Jesus took your place and position so that you could take His place in favor, seated at the right hand of God.

When you begin to see yourself seated in Christ at the right hand of God, your heart will find true rest. You will begin to be amazed by the doors that open for you when you didn't even make an effort to open them. There is a rhythm of grace and an effortless path to blessing found in His favor.

Be still and know that I am God, I will be exalted among the nations, I will be exalted in the earth! (Psalm 46:10).

Psalm 46:10 is a verse you might've heard before, but I want you to take note of the first four words: "Be still and know." In our culture, we do mostly the opposite of what this verse is saying. In our world today, it's pretty much "Keep moving, and make sure you take care of everything yourself, otherwise you'll fall behind." This way of thinking causes us to constantly look to ourselves, our effort, our ability, and our position; but His words and His ways are always drawing our eyes back to Him.

To "be still and know" requires that we stop leaning on

our own effort, which is oftentimes why it's hard for us to be still. For some reason, we seem to think we can accomplish more than God can for us. We'd often rather strive for things, instead of letting Him give them to us in His perfect timing.

Friend, being still and knowing that He is God is not "doing nothing." The enemy of your mind may lie to you and tell you, "You're doing nothing"; but trusting and knowing that He is God is the MOST productive thing you could do. He is the God who parts the waters for you, who sets your feet on solid ground. He leads you in paths of righteousness for His name's sake. You can be still and know that HE is your favor. ◊

Jesus *took your place and position so that you could take His place in favor.*

DECLARATION *Prayer*

Jesus, You Are My Favor.

I choose to rest in Your hand, knowing You have surrounded me with favor. I choose today to be still and know that You are my God. You have seated me in Christ with every blessing in heavenly places. I will not strive to earn, but I will rest and receive from You all that You have waiting for me. You are beyond faithful and better than I could ever dream. Thank You, Jesus, for this gift. In Jesus' name; Amen.

JESUS
My Defender

---

*So when they continued
asking Him, He raised Himself
up and said to them, "He who
is without sin among you, let
him throw a stone at her first."*

JOHN 8:7 NKJV

F riend, you don't have to defend yourself. Jesus is your great Defender. Look at the story of the woman caught in adultery in John 8. In the very act of sin, in the middle of being caught and accused, Jesus came and stood by her side. Jesus came to the woman's rescue and was her only defense.

The amazing thing about Jesus is that He doesn't defend us based on our goodness or our innocence; Jesus defends us based on the position we have been given in Him. Even in the middle of committing adultery, Jesus counted the woman righteous and worthy of being free. This is the kind of defender and friend you want to have around: the kind that comes to your defense, who sees what you're capable of, who empowers you to change, and sets you free. Jesus is the Defender of your heart. When the enemy comes to accuse, remind you of the past, or condemn your heart, Jesus will be your Defender. When co-workers, family members, or friends misunderstand you, Jesus will be your Defender. Even if the whole world were to pick up their stones and aim them at you, HE would still come to your side as your great Defender.

Just like Moses told the Israelites when he was leading them out of Egypt, "The LORD will fight for you, and you shall hold your peace" (Exodus 14:14). You can rest in knowing that He will fight for you, and you need only to be still. He is defending you and leading you to all that He has for you.

Be still and see Him fight, defend, and deliver you from your enemies. He will speak for and stand by you just like He did for the woman who was surrounded by her accusers. And He will let you go free, no matter the accusation. ◊

DECLARATION *Prayer*

Jesus, You Are My Defender.

Today, I will be still and let You defend and fight for me. Thank You for defending me, not based on my own goodness but based on Your goodness and righteousness. No matter what may come in life, I can always rest knowing that You are my Defender. You are the One who stands by me, speaks for me, and sets me free from all my accusers. Thank You, Jesus!

JESUS
My Salvation

———————

*For by grace you have been saved
through faith, and that not of
yourselves; it is the gift of God, not
of works, lest anyone should boast.*

EPHESIANS 2:8–9 NKJV

The word *salvation* by definition means, "the act of saving or protecting from harm, risk, loss, destruction, etc." For us, this act was done by Jesus, once and for ALL time.

Though many of us may know salvation came through Jesus, somehow, we still find ourselves questioning whether or not we are truly "saved," or if we can lose our salvation. Somehow it seems that once we come to Jesus and receive salvation, we begin to think the rest of our lives is up to us. Without even realizing it, we can see salvation as a one-time transaction for one moment of our lives, instead of realizing that salvation is a gift for the rest of our lives.

Salvation for the believer is based on faith. To receive salvation, it takes a person simply "believing" in Jesus for the salvation from their sins. So why then after that point do we begin looking to ourselves for our salvation? For some reason, we suddenly we think it's up to us to be good, holy, righteous, and ultimately, like Jesus. But friend, when did Jesus say this? When did Jesus say once you're saved, now this salvation is up to you?

The good news is, He didn't.

The good news is good because it's all about Jesus; all the focus is on Him, not on us.

Romans 5:17 says,

> For if, by the trespass of the one man, death reigned through that one man, how much more will those who receive God's abundant provision of grace and of the gift of righteousness reign in life through the one man, Jesus Christ! (NIV).

Friend, your salvation started with His abundant provision of grace and His GIFT of righteousness, and it will end with the same. The enemy of your soul will constantly try to make you doubt your position in Christ and the grace on which it was established. You must know this so that when the enemy points you to your failures, you can point him to Jesus. ◊

The good news is good because it's all about Jesus; *all the focus is on Him, not on us.*

DECLARATION *Prayer*

Jesus, You Are My Salvation.
I receive Your abundant grace and GIFT of righteousness. My salvation is not of works or my own doing, but simply by faith in Your name. I thank You that Your gift of salvation was not just for one day, but forever. In Jesus' name; Amen.

JESUS
My Safe Place

---

*When you sit enthroned under the
shadow of Shaddai, you are hidden
in the strength of God Most High.
He's the hope that holds me and the
Stronghold to shelter me, the only
God for me, and my great confidence.*

PSALM 91:1–2 TPT

L ife is full of the unexpected, but nothing comes as a surprise to Jesus. Just as He recorded every day of your life in His book before a single moment had passed, He recorded each moment full of His faithfulness, goodness, and protection for you.

When you sit enthroned under the shadow of Shaddai,
you are hidden in the strength of God Most High.
He's the hope that holds me and the Stronghold to shelter me,
the only God for me, and my great confidence.
He will rescue you from every hidden trap of the enemy,
and he will protect you from false accusation
and any deadly curse.
His massive arms are wrapped around you, protecting you.
You can run under his covering of majesty and hide.
His arms of faithfulness are a shield keeping you from harm.
You will never worry about an attack of demonic forces at night
nor have to fear a spirit of darkness coming against you.
Don't fear a thing!
Whether by night or by day, demonic danger
will not trouble you,
nor will the powers of evil launched against you.
Even in a time of disaster, with thousands and
thousands being killed,
you will remain unscathed and unharmed.
you will be a spectator as the wicked perish in judgment,
for they will be paid back for what they have done!
When we live our lives within the shadow of God Most High,

our secret hiding place, we will always be shielded from harm.
How then could evil prevail against us or disease infect us?
God sends angels with special orders to protect you
wherever you go,
defending you from all harm.
If you walk into a trap, they'll be there for you
and keep you from stumbling.
You'll even walk unharmed among the fiercest
powers of darkness,
trampling every one of them beneath your feet!
For here is what the Lord has spoken to me:
"Because you have delighted in me as my great lover,
I will greatly protect you.
I will set you in a high place, safe and secure before my face.
I will answer your cry for help every time you pray,
and you will find and feel my presence
even in your time of pressure and trouble.
I will be your glorious hero and give you a feast.
You will be satisfied with a full life and with all that I do for you.
For you will enjoy the fullness of my salvation!"
(Psalm 91, TPT).

Whether the battle is visible or invisible, Jesus promises to protect you. Delight in His protection and His great love, and let Him do what He longs to do in your life. ◊

DECLARATION *Prayer*

Jesus, You Are My Safe Place.
No matter where I am, I know that I can run under Your covering of majesty and hide. You are the hope that holds me and the stronghold that shelters me. You are my great confidence. I trust in You to protect me in every moment and shield me from all harm. I am safe and secure before Your face. Thank you. In Jesus' name; Amen.

LANEY RENE

JESUS

My Teacher

───────────

Jesus said to him, "I am the way, the truth, and the life. No one comes to the Father except through Me."

JOHN 14:6 NKJV

Do you ever read the Bible and think, *This is so confusing?* Unless we understand the context of what is going on in different parts of the Bible, we might think the Bible is constantly contradicting itself.

The first half of the Bible (Old Testament) speaks of a Savior to come but is still based on law. The second half of the Bible (New Testament) is when Jesus comes, but up until the crucifixion Jesus was still giving the law. The law has a purpose. The law is not void once we receive Jesus, but the law allows us to see our need for Jesus and the full purpose of why He came.

Many times, we think the Bible is confusing because we read it all the same. We must understand that the whole Bible is pointing us to the Savior. The whole Bible is meant to point us to Jesus; and if we don't look for Him when we read His Word, we could easily miss the whole point!

If we truly understand what Jesus came to do, this will completely change how we read any part of Scripture.

Jesus came to do many things—one of those things was to fulfill the law. If the law were never fulfilled, you and I would still be under the law. But, Jesus' life, crucifixion, and resurrection was the fulfillment of the law.

John 19:28–30 says,

> *After this, Jesus, knowing that all things were now accomplished, that the Scripture might be fulfilled, said, "I thirst!" Now a vessel full of sour wine was sitting there; and they filled a sponge with sour wine, put it on hyssop,*

and put it to His mouth. So when Jesus had received the
sour wine, He said, "It is finished!" And bowing His head,
He gave up His spirit.

When you read your Bible, one of the simplest yet pro-found things to remember is this: "It is finished." You must read your Bible through the lens of completion. The law was a list of do's and don'ts that were meant to show us what we could not do on our own, which then leads us to understand the fullness of what was done for us. Allow yourself, when you begin reading, to look for Jesus and in doing this you will learn a whole new way to read His Word. If you begin to see your weaknesses, allow the Word to lift your eyes to the power of His blood. Everything in His Word is meant to point to Him.

When Jesus left the earth, He sent us the Helper, the Holy Spirit. John 14:26 says, ". . . He will teach you all things, and bring to your remembrance all things that I [Jesus] said to you." You have a Helper when you open the Word, who is there to help you understand and point you to Jesus. He will be your Teacher, and He will show you what is true of Himself. ◊

DECLARATION *Prayer*

Jesus, You Are My Teacher.

I look to You today for understanding of Your Word. I thank You that You are not the author of confusion. I ask You to help me always read through the lens of completion. Thank You for redeeming me from the law and its requirements. My faith is built on what You finished for me. Thank You, Jesus!

JESUS
My Evidence

. . .being confident of this, that he who began a good work in you will carry it on to completion until the day of Christ Jesus.

PHILIPPIANS 1:6, NIV

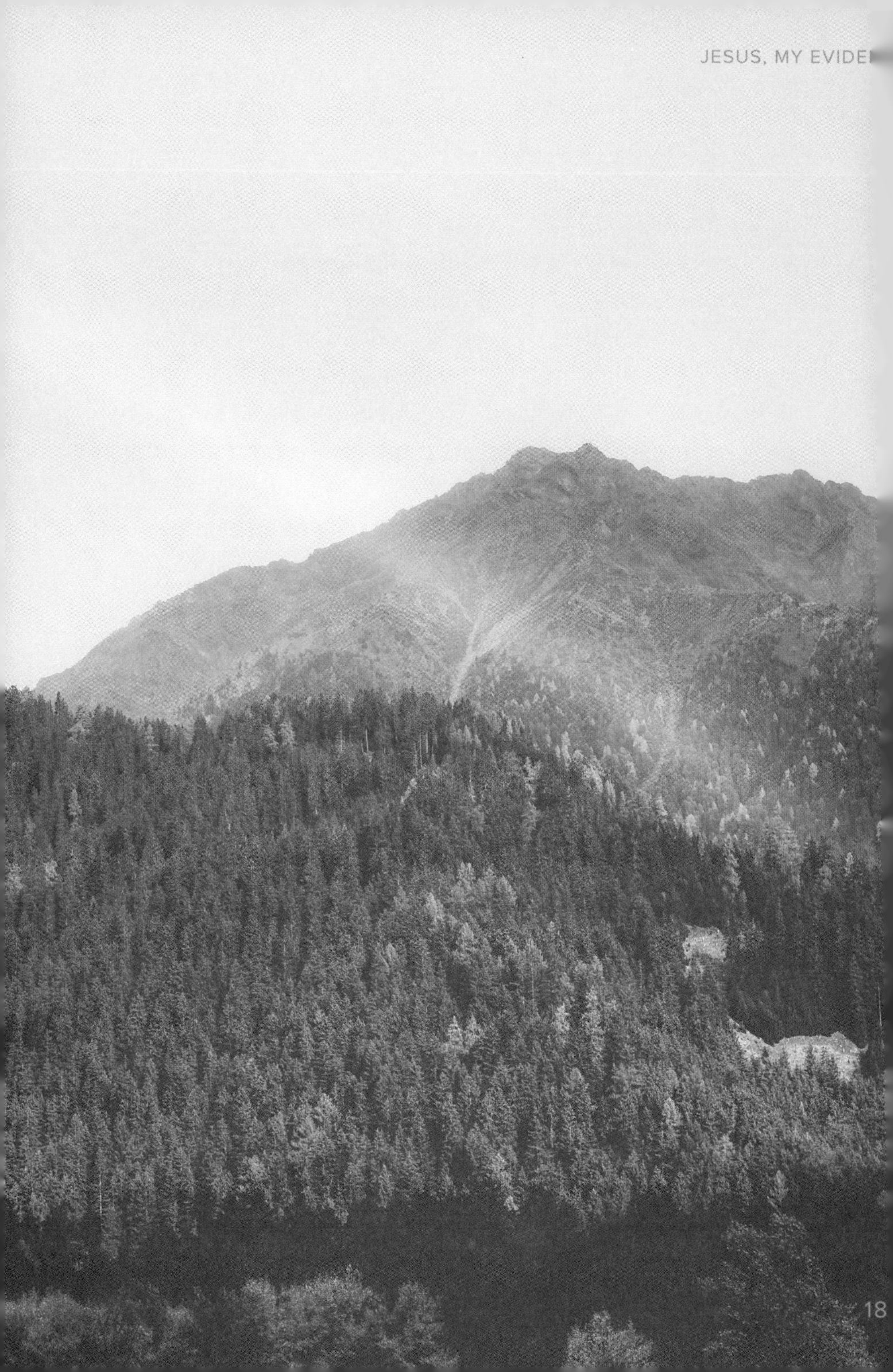

Abraham was one hundred years old when he received his promised son, Isaac. Sarah gave birth to her promised son when she was *past* the age of childbearing. Joseph was betrayed by his own brothers and sold into slavery before he became second in command of *all* Egypt. The walls of Jericho didn't fall until the seventh day that the people marched around them. Mary and Martha's brother, Lazarus, remained dead for four days before God brought him back to life. Jesus didn't rise from the dead until the third day.

What if Abraham stopped believing God's promise at ninety-nine because he thought he was too old? What if Sarah never believed she would have a son because the circumstances didn't look too promising? Imagine if they would have stopped believing one week earlier. Imagine how hard it must've been for them to believe what God had promised them. I imagine that there wasn't much for them to see with their eyes to give them faith to believe. The physical evidence of the promise was nonexistent up until the miracle happened, but God's voice was not absent. God was very present, and His promise was the fuel to their faith and the evidence for the things not yet seen. One week potentially could've changed everything for them, but instead it says, "because Sarah judged Him faithful who had promised," she was able to conceive and give birth to a child (Hebrews 11:11).

If God has given you a promise, don't look for your evidence in the things around you. Don't wait for someone to tell you you're doing the right thing or for the approval of another person. People may not always understand everything you're doing, and that is okay! Not everyone is meant to understand the path that you're on, not even you.

Hebrews 11:8 tells us that faith is what motivated Abraham to leave the familiar to discover the territory he was destined to inherit from God. He left with only a promise, "not knowing where he was going." You may not know exactly where you're going, but you can have full confidence that GOD does. Follow His peace and let faith be your evidence. Find the encouragement you need in His Word and trust His character. He will never stop being faithful. Just as He was faithful to Abraham and Sarah, He WILL be faithful to you. Things are not always what they seem, so you must look with eyes of faith. See the name of Jesus covering everything in your world: your family, your job, your finances, and your future.

Hebrews 11:13 (TPT) says, ". . . But they saw beyond the horizon the fulfillment of their promises and gladly embraced it from afar. They all lived their lives on earth as those who belonged to another realm." Sometimes, something can look so perfect and seem so right, but you just might not have peace about it. And sometimes, something can completely not make sense looking at it from the outside, but you can have a perfect peace that it is right. Faith doesn't always make sense, but the Bible tells us that it is the "foundation needed to acquire the things we long for. It is all the evidence required to prove what is still unseen" (Hebrews 11:1, TPT). So let your faith be your evidence today. Keep believing because you know that He is faithful to complete what He started. ◊

DECLARATION *Prayer*

Jesus, You Are My Evidence.

You are the One promise that I choose to put all my hope and trust in. I thank You that You have always been faithful and will always be faithful. I trust that, just like You provided for Abraham and Sarah, You will provide for me in Your perfect timing. Jesus, Your faithfulness is all the evidence I need to keep going and keep believing. You will never let me down. In Your name I pray. Thank You, Jesus!